Southern Voices

Fifty Contemporary Poets

Southern Voices

Fifty Contemporary Poets

edited by

Tom Mack

and

Andrew Geyer

LITERARY PRESS
LAMAR UNIVERSITY

ISBN: 978-1-962148-13-9
Library of Congress Control Number: 2024943844
Manufactured in the United States

Cover Design: Katie Hoerth
Front Cover Painting: *Pine Log Road* by Michael Budd, BFA

The editors gratefully acknowledge the generous and continuing support of the James L. and Mary W. Oswald Endowment and the Oswald family.

CONTENTS

COVER ARTIST

EDITORS

INTRODUCTION

The Voices of the South

TOM MACK

There is no exact English equivalent for the Spanish word "querencia," but some translate the term to mean "the place where a person is their most authentic self." For the fifty contemporary poets in this unique volume, that place is the American South, from the East Coast to the Ozarks.

Place means more, of course, than simply the physical environment. In scanning this anthology's many fine selections, nevertheless, readers will confront palpable evocations of the topography, atmosphere, flora, and fauna of the Southern United States. Appalachian poet Ron Rash, for example, conjures up images of Black-eyed Susans as mountaintop memento mori; Jim Minick notes the behavior of grackles as they pause on their way "to nest in saltmarshes soon gone to flood." Coastal poet Libby Bernardin responds lyrically to "the beat of deep rhythmic tides," and Robert Morgan registers the "electric display" of a summer thunderstorm that can "whip roots out of steaming ground."

In his poem "Postcards from Arkansas," Ed Madden asks, "What landscape do you carry inside you?" Campbell McGrath, for one, reimagines the Everglades as a "paradise of flocks, a cornucopia of wind and grass and dark, slow waters" while Kentucky Poet Laureate Silas House remembers penetrating the "darksome cavern" tucked behind Cumberland Falls, a "secret cathedral made of wildness and wet." Jerry Craven relives the moment he spread a blanket "on sand beside desert water falling into the heat of a Texas summer," and Amanda Rachelle Warren observes how a "fine mist dulls the gloss of magnolia" on a Carolina night.

As Joey Brown notes in her poem "Limnology," "how we wear place," how we express the lived experience of the Southern landscape, can take many forms. This volume's rich assortment of lyrical responses to the hills and mountains, swamps and beaches, verdant river valleys and fertile agricultural expanses of the South can, for example, very often morph into narrative.

So much has been written about the Southern storytelling tradition, and one can discover this penchant for spinning yarns in all the art forms of this region, from painting to poetry. Thus, Ron Smith's "Running Again in Hollywood Cemetery" not only offers the reader detailed descriptions of this iconic Confederate burying ground in Richmond, Virginia, but also resurrects the poet's memories of his youthful, hormone-infused misadventures in that place. Youthful exuberance remains the order of the day in Travis Denton's "Inertia and the Past in All Its Glory" as the poet reminisces about cruising down Peachtree Street, Atlanta's iconic downtown thoroughfare, in a 1968 convertible. In describing a dory under a tarp in a friend's yard, Edward Wilson pays homage to a man who devoted countless hours refurbishing a vessel he would himself never take to sea; and both Cathy Smith Bowers and Jo Angela Edwins venture deeply into tall-tale territory with their poetic treatments of zombie voters and atomic bomb "accidents."

A quick perusal of this volume makes clear, therefore, that the South can be defined not just by its location on the map. It is also a state of mind. Consider, in this regard, John Lane's paeon to the quintessential Southern drink: "For God so loved the world she made sweet tea." The taste of the South also shares printed space with its sounds. Roy Seeger's poem "Amanda's in the Backyard, Plucking at the Banjo" extols the "comfort" to be found in a Bluegrass song. For Marcus Amaker, the first poet laureate of Charleston, South Carolina, one musical form of distinctly Southern origin provides the soundtrack for his daily life: "the steady beat of jazz is the beat of [the] streets."

Much has also been written about how much the weight of history can be felt in the American South. This abiding presence of the past can be ascribed partially to folk traditions, many of which can be linked to ancestral practice, particularly customs brought to the

2

Southern states from Africa. Lyman Grant celebrates, for example, the Southern phenomenon of the bottle tree and the magical luminescence that results "when the moon is full and its stark eye sparkles the dark cobalt glass." The sight of a bank of red clay reminds Carolina poet Glenis Redmond of a story her mother once told her of harvesting and ingesting soil, an inherited cultural practice sometimes used as a countermeasure to digestive problems; Alabama Poet Laureate Ashley M. Jones does Redmond one better by personally eating red clay with her Aunt Hattie, her "Southern pride" overcoming her aversion to the "strange, dull sour scent."

Then there is the matter of spiritual faith, which is often passed down in families from generation to generation. Summoning up "old blood ties," Ron Rash pays homage to his roots and the "hardshell Baptists, farmers who believed the soul is another seed that endures when flesh and blood are shed." Gilbert Allen provides a fresh perspective on the covenant of grace in "The Heaven of Mistaken Assumptions," and Robert Morgan offers readers commentary on the "celebrity status" of that arch-betrayer Judas.

However Biblically minded most Southerners may be, the contemporary life of the spirit in this region is not confined solely to one path. Some, like the North Carolina poet Gavin Dillard, have broken their ties to their more traditional upbringing. In one of his short quasi-oracular verses, for example, Dillard tells readers that he can hear the Voice in "the quietest of times," and not necessarily when he is repeating a mantra in accordance with the Buddhist practice of Japa.

Along with faith, another factor binding many Southerners together is a focus on the family in all its permutations, both positive and negative. On one hand, for example, there are Denise Duhamel's loving tributes to her late mother, in poignant memories triggered in turn by a yellow shirt and a teal-blue cover-up; and Jo Angela Edwins's imagining how her mother must have coped when as a child she helped to clear out the family homestead when her Tennessee valley was flooded after the construction of a high dam. In contrast, there is Georgia Poet Laureate Chelsea Rathburn's poetic pondering about whether "life (is) just a series of torments and obligations," the result of having to visit as a child her grandparents in their "dismal single-wide" every July.

Perhaps no other region of this vast country is haunted more by the past. In the case of the American South, heavy lie the legacy of

3

slavery and the specter of the Civil War. Terrance Hayes, for instance, reminds the reader of how the term "buy one, get one free" may have been uttered by slave traders "when pregnant African girls mounted the auction block." In "Charleston Rooftops," Marjory Wentworth writes of the devastating consequences of the city's role in defense of the slave economy: "odors of ruin and rot lingered in the air above the streets emptied by war; the bells silent in the steeples." That very same "ruin" the animate statue of Robert E. Lee in Lyman Grant's poem "Pedestal" acknowledges to be the result of a collective moral lapse: "I'm not a hero for someone's lost cause. Take me down. Let truth march on."

Yet, the winds of change can be felt throughout the American South, due in large part to both a generational and demographic shift—the region is consistently being enriched by transplants from other parts of the country and other nations of the world. Louisa A. Igloria, a native of the Philippines, for example, recently served as Virginia's Poet Laureate.

Although Igloria writes in "A Commonwealth" that she does not often see others whose faces resemble hers and that perhaps "dark-skinned ones . . . are careful to avoid spaces where rebel flags with seven stars still whip in the wind," change is coming to the South. Heretofore marginalized voices are slowly being heard, and impassioned dissent is not uncommon. In this volume, readers will find calls for political and social equality regardless of race, gender, or sexual orientation. Outrage against an unbridled gun culture and pleas for responsible environmental stewardship have also found their way onto these pages.

In "Why I Write Poems," Marcus Amaker insists that "writing a poem is world building." Let us hope that the world in question acknowledges, in the words of Marjory Wentworth in "One River, One Boat," that we are "huddled together on this boat handed down to us—stuck at the last bend of a wide river splintering near the sea"—and that it is incumbent on all of us to row together to reach the hoped-for safety of some promised shore.

The Greater South:
A Note on the Text and Those Who Created It

ANDREW GEYER

Greater South. What does that term truly signify?

To my own mind's inner compass, "Greater South" seems almost a contradiction in terms: after all, what is the South if not "the opposite of the North; the place that lies below the East and the West?" The answer is . . . well, truth be told, it's complicated. But I challenge anyone to give that question a better answer than the contents of this book.

The fifty contemporary poets who were invited to contribute work to *Southern Voices* have each put their own unique spin on what makes the South be what it is at this moment, in the year 2024, almost a quarter of the way through the new century that is unfolding around us. The poems in this exciting volume crisscross the Greater American South from Virginia to the Ozarks, from the Texas hill country to the Florida coast, exploring—in a variety of forms and on an amazing array of subjects—all the corners of this continually evolving region including its flora, fauna, cultural idiosyncrasies, dark history, and distinctive cuisines.

But with regard to lines drawn on a map, intrepid readers who venture into the poems collected here will vicariously visit the states of Alabama, Arkansas, Florida, Georgia, Kentucky, Louisiana, Mississippi, Missouri, North Carolina, Oklahoma, South Carolina, Tennessee, Texas, Virginia, and West Virginia.

Why these particular states, some may ask, and not others? Why not Delaware, for example, or Maryland? Why these particular poets, and not others? Did you limit invitations to native Southerners, or did you let in those who migrated to the Greater South from less fortunate points of origin? The remainder of my introduction will be dedicated to answering those questions, and some others, while hopefully whetting the appetites of prospective readers for the literary feast that follows.

I'll begin by using as a case study the well-traveled editors who put this volume together, and then I'll move on to discussing various elements of the gorgeous poems it has been our great good fortune to include between its covers.

My current editorial partner in crime, former department chair, and longtime dear friend, Tom Mack, is one of the contributors to this book who migrated to the Greater South from less fortunate points of origin. Having begun his life and spent the majority of his formative years in the state of Pennsylvania, Dr. Mack came to South Carolina to teach American literature—and soon thereafter to chair the Department of English—at the University of South Carolina Aiken. He has since come to play an integral role in the literary life and artistic legacy of the state he has come to call home.

As for myself, I was born in Austin, lived briefly in Louisiana, and then grew up on a working cattle ranch in Southwest Texas. I was stationed in Georgia and North Carolina when I served in the US Army, attended graduate school in South Carolina and Texas, and served as an English professor in South Carolina, Oklahoma, Texas, Arkansas, and again in South Carolina. I am a member of the Texas Institute of Letters and the South Carolina Academy of Authors. So although I rightly call myself a native Southerner, to which state do I truly belong?

I think the safest answer is *all of the above.*

When we set about putting together an anthology of contemporary Southern poetry, Tom and I were determined to be as broadly inclusive as possible within the page limit set by the press. We settled on fifty as the number of poets whose work we hoped to feature in our volume and chose *place* and *voice* as particular thematic elements that we hoped each poet would address in their poems. In other words, we decided to let half a hundred wordsmiths forge their own composite definition of the term "Greater South" in the smithy of their own poetic sensibilities. The result is this book.

As place and voice were most particularly on our minds, we quickly hit upon the idea of inviting poets-laureate at both the state and municipal levels—artists whose works had been selected by the members of their own communities as best representing the qualities by which those communities defined themselves—as the truest way to make this volume most broadly inclusive of those who think of themselves as Southern. A quick perusal of the biographies that follow will serve as a testament to the willingness of those poets-laureate to share such representative works with our audience. Additionally, both Tom and I—as a function of serving as the English Department Chair at USC Aiken—have spent years directing the James and Mary Oswald

Distinguished Writers Series at USCA. The series has as its primary focus the works of Southern authors, and many of the poets included in this volume were invited based on the excellence of their contributions as Oswald Distinguished Writing Fellows.

The term "Southern" is one that comes with a bundle of expectations. One of the things I expected when inviting the contributions of poets-laureate from states and cities across the South was that the poems we received would be set exclusively in that particular piece of the South each poet was selected to represent. I must confess myself most delightfully surprised by the wide variety of poetic destinations that are visited in this anthology. Indeed, one of the primary characteristics of the Greater South in the year 2024 as defined by the fifty poets in *Southern Voices* is that it is continually in motion. The kinds of movement captured by the poems in this volume include things physical, spiritual, gustatory, ontological, historical, and meteorological. Indeed, my advice to you, dear reader, as you explore the poems that follow is to expect the unexpected.

Enjoy.

POETS & POEMS

GILBERT ALLEN grew up on Long Island and earned BA, MFA, and PhD degrees from Cornell University, where he was a Ford Foundation Fellow. Since 1977 he has lived in Travelers Rest, South Carolina, with his wife, the educator and environmental activist Barbara Allen. He has published seven collections of poems (most recently *Believing in Two Bodies*) and two collections of linked short stories (most recently *The Beasts of Belladonna*). In 2018 he edited *Archive: South Carolina Poetry Since 2005* with Jeffrey Makala and William E. Rogers. Gilbert Allen's honors include the Robert Penn Warren Prize from *The Southern Review*, special mention for a Pushcart Prize, and election to the South Carolina Academy of Authors. He became the Bennette E. Geer Professor of Literature Emeritus at Furman University upon his early retirement from teaching in 2015.

Acknowledgments

"Two Become One Flesh"
> First published in *The Southern Review*. Featured on *Poetry Daily* (August 17, 2016) and reprinted in *Believing in Two Bodies* (Kelsay Books, 2020)

"Clearcut"
> First published in *Appalachian Journal*

"For the Lost Fathers"
> First published in *EPOCH*

Clearcut

Travelers Rest, South Carolina

Nothing's left standing to see.
Morning rain makes a melody
of mud in this sawdusted city
of stumps—every tree harvested
for next season's firewood,
newspapers, novels,
bungalows, barrels.

Still, it seems almost greening
walking here in the waning
weeks of winter, gleaning
what will become of what was
from only the nothing that is—
in the new afterlife
someone will find enough.

Invitation

Good morning, Neighbors!

Those of you
who have been looking forward to
our Ladies Shooting Spree tonight
please text or email so I might
reserve a dedicated lane
at City Arsenal (off Main).

If need be, you can rent a gun—
I'd recommend a Remington.

The targets are $1.00 per—
imagine they're adulterers!
Or bring your own, if you'd prefer.

Come as you are. No special dress.
So glad you guys can make it!

Tess

Two Become One Flesh

with apologies to Mark 10:8

He can't hoist either hand above his head.
Her feet won't stand more than a dozen steps.
He's too nearsighted for the DMV.
Her fingers feel like she's got mittens on.
When did his legs get too long for his arms?
When did her arms get too short for her eyes?
He can't smell newsprint pressed against his nose.
She can't hear *Thanks* while helping with his socks.

The kitchen bulb burns out for both and each.

She drives the car. He strides into Best Buy.
Back home, he brings the stool. She stretches high.
He shouts the recipe. She bakes the quiche.
He listens for the *ding*. She finds the plates.
He cuts. They eat. She tells him how it tastes.

For the Lost Fathers

Today I'm vacuuming the bedroom carpet—
long overdue—with all the loose furniture
lifted aside, the floor empty as my mind
could make it. I look toward the bureau bookcase
at the Polaroid of my father, pretending
to play an upright piano—a silly gag
a few years before he died—while the word
forgotten seems to breathe from the machine
as if it were a solitary lung
laboring after sixty years of smoking.

I turn it off. I'm one of the few alive
who know his hands couldn't find the middle *C*.
So I can't help imagining this image
beheld by others, centuries from now—
the future holding music visible
but never there. A silent lie. And then

the picture itself, dissolving into dust,
or mold, or fire, within a world that has
forgotten Polaroids, and me, and must
and will forget every last one of us.

I turn the vacuum on, get back to work

and find, next to my father, the blue spine
of Jim McConkey's *Court of Memory*,
concluded by "What Kind of Father Am I?"

And in an unrehearsed *recitativo*
both men insist: *Fathers will be forgotten.*
But the present always will recall,
remember someone now not of this world—
who once recalled, in his or her own turn,
another being from a world more distant.

Invisible minds holding invisible hands
across the great courtyard of time itself
that does and will reach to infinity
in both directions, making the universe
once and for all whole as the mind of God.

The Heaven of Mistaken Assumptions

*Behold, there appeared a chariot of fire, and horses of fire, and
separated them, and Elijah went up by a whirlwind into heaven.*
—2 Kings 2:11

Here are all God's mistakes:
the Adolphs, the Evas,
Benito, Iago, the Duke
of Ferrara—the actual
and those imagined
by His better creations—
gathered together in this cacophony
of clouds and miserable manna
waiting for grace.

Which arrives, albeit
in modest measure. For even
these who have labored
under their dark, dire
assumptions have been assumed
to this special, if segregated, space.

What did You expect, My Son?

Who replies He was almost human
like them, once, yet not forsaken

while the Holy Ghost, nodding,
gazes with something akin to affection
at all those immaculate white robes—
even the ones with hoods.

MARCUS AMAKER (he/him) takes daily naps and is Charleston, South Carolina's first poet laureate. He's also an opera librettist, an electronic musician, and an award-winning graphic designer. He's an Academy of American Poets fellow, and his poetry has been recognized by NPR, the *Washington Post*, *Pittsburgh Post-Gazette*, *Garden & Gun*, the Kennedy Center, and more. His tenth book is *Hold What Makes You Whole*, from Free Verse Press. His original opera with composer Gillian Rae Perry, *The Weight of Light*, premiered at the Chicago Opera Theater in 2024. His 40th album, *a machine & its threads*, was released by Sufriemento Records, an electronic music label based in Buenos Aires, Argentina.

Acknowledgments

"Retelling and the Remembering"
    First published in *The Birth of All Things* (Free Verse Press)
"Why I Write Poems," "The Pulse," and "Gerridae (Self-Portrait, Part 5)"
    First published in *Hold What Makes You Whole* (Free Verse Press)

Retelling and the Remembering

Black spirits can not be absent
from anything. Especially in South Carolina,

where every open, abandoned space
holds a family's erased echo,

and racism is embedded in every
memory. We, the living, have the privilege
of being

restful ghosts. We haunt material
things, and hold our history in excess.
But here,

and everywhere around us, we walk
among the haunted. An old house can not
be entered

without touching its nostalgia. An untold
story is an unmarked grave waiting for
revision.

This is why we preserve what was once
condemned: To put fresh ink on faded text
and to remember that we can't erase each other.

The Pulse

We live in Charleston!

Where the sidewalks scream
on Saturday nights
and the corners rotate
budding musicians
with skin-tight dreams,

where strings of pearls
search for salvation
then sweat out their frustrations
on the backs of rooftops,

where the homeless sprout
like weeds through concrete
seeking two dollars, a handshake
and a little bit of sunshine,

where the humidity
chokes you out of your breath
but you still manage to speak to the spit-shine waiters
who serve $95 bottles of wine,

where two blocks away,
a $5 pitcher of liquid gold
spills on the canvas of sticky floors,

where love lingers on cobblestone streets
in narrow alleyways,
but the smell of sex
is the foundation
for first and last impressions.

We live in Charleston!

Where shadows are surrounded
by the ocean
and sea-seeing people gasp for air
from knee-deep bills
and dirt-cheap thrills,

where those with
no sense of history's melody
sync with the songs of the city's slaves,

where the poets scrape stanzas
off of streetlights
and if they scream loud enough
maybe someone won't be afraid of the dark.

I live in Charleston!

Where church steeples and cranes
look over us
and multicolored houses
house live-in servants,
where fast-rising hotels
rise above slow-moving clouds
that cast floods on the corner
of America Street,

where parades of one color
get one day to celebrate
then hide in the shadows
of gentrification,

where Gullah cuisine
is too expensive
for Gullah people.

The Holy City!

Where the steady beat of jazz
is the beat of our streets
and the dialect of our past
writes future conversations,

where bridges and bike lanes
break bread with politics,
while some of us preach peace
with uneducated tongues.

Where the Angel Oak tree is young
compared to our vanity,
where $16 burgers
are sold in the middle of a food desert
while every community
wants a piece of the pie.

Where grandmothers sit on porches,
watching us change
while the problems of our city
remain the same.

We live in Charleston!

Where the ghosts and yoga studios
call themselves "holy"
and the vintage market calls itself "holy"
and the whiskey drinkers go to church
to feel tender and holy,

where potholes and potheads
blow smoke through steam-filled summers,
and the pandemic was brushed away
like palmetto bugs laughing in the face of death.

Where some of us dream
of an underground scene
to hold on to the spirit of elevation,

where halter tops don't stop in the winter
for people with disposable incomes
and opposable thumbs.

The Holy City.

Where the hurricanes are coming,
where the hurricanes are coming,
where the hurricanes are coming.

Another Charleston is being built
above our heads.

Maybe that one won't flood?

"Why I Write Poems"

Because I can't say my last name
to a stranger without stuttering.
Because written words will age
and change tone with time.
Because my speaking voice will
eventually go silent.
Because my pen is as dark as my mind.
Because when there's a gnat in my cocktail
I wonder if it had a death wish.
Because I think about the history
and intention of insects.
Because I wonder if house keys
go into hiding on purpose.
Because sometimes I, too, want to
stay secluded when I am lost.
Because poetry opens doors.
Because writing a poem is world building.
Because it insists I work on the things
I've been resisting.
Because a sharp turn of phrase
can sting like the edge of a blunt piece of paper.

Gerridae (Self Portrait, Part 5)

I'm here to honor all parts of myself:

The man who is scared of death
but romanticizes heaven,

the warrior who would kill for his daughter
then stays up all night spooked by shadows,

the fire-driven miracle seeker
who pretends to rise above everything,

the hot mess.

The punk rocker,

the full-grown gentleman who cries
when watching *Star Wars* cartoons.

A descendent of sassafras drinkers.
Of collards, cabbage, and black-eyed peas
in Orangeburg, South Carolina.

I'm here to honor every version of myself:

The teenager who was too embarrassed
to tell his friends he wrote poetry,

the sour adult who is proud
that his muse has the confidence of honey,

the polymath and the
adrenaline avalanche of youth,

the body that is well on its way to decay,

the empath who water-skips through life
but is afraid to go under.

I'm here to give grace to everything I am:

To lay a blanket next to the grave
of my former selves,

and sit among seeds that were
never meant to flourish,

and dig up reminders of how
I've come to be in bloom.

ALAN BERECKA grew up in rural Central New York. He came to Texas in 1977 to attend the University of Dallas. For many years he earned his keep as a librarian at Del Mar College in Corpus Christi. He retired in 2023 and currently resides in Sinton, Texas, with his wife Alice and an ornery rescue dog named Ophelia. His poems have appeared in such publications as *The Christian Century, The American Literary Review, The Texas Review,* and *The Concho River Review.* He has authored six collections of poetry. The latest book, *Atlas Sighs: Selected and New Poems,* was published by Turning Plow Press in 2024. From 2017-2019 he served as the first poet laureate of Corpus Christi, TX. In 2022 he was a guest of the Lithuanian Writer's Union and participated in their festival throughout Lithuania.

Acknowledgments

"Commuting"
> First published in *Windhover* and reprinted in *Atlas Sighs: Selected and New Poems* (Turning Plow Press, 2024)

"Hearing of Uvalde While Visiting Vilnius" and "Mastering the Local Dialect"
> First published in the *Texas Poetry Assignment* and reprinted in *Atlas Sighs: Selected and New Poems* (Turning Plow Press, 2024)

"A Transplant Speaks" and "Out of Our Depths"
> First published in *Atlas Sighs: Selected and New Poems* (Turning Plow Press, 2024)

A Transplant Speaks

My wife has no talent for horticulture.
Every gifted plant she ever received
found itself on death row, condemned
to wither to a slow death, executed
by what she calls her *black thumbs*.

I grew up in a verdant northern valley
beneath ancient pines and maples.
Recently, I entered a confused state
caused by a sort of identity crisis
brought on by an invitation to submit
to an anthology of Southern writers.

Nonplussed, my wife, once a military brat,
who was born in South Dakota from folks
who called Missouri home but ended up in Dallas,
told me, "Do the math. For two-thirds of your life,
you have lived in Texas." She reminded me
that I studied at its universities and added
that we met and were married in Texas,
that our children were born and raised here,
that we have decided to retire and stay here
and asked, "So why shouldn't you be a Texan?"

A few years back, my wife brought home
a few hopeless-looking green sticks.
"They're Plumeria," she claimed, placing
them each in its own large ceramic pot.
I laughed, but in spite of their presumed fate
the sticks flourished, bloomed, and multiplied.
Our back patio now resembles a flowering forest.

Shallow root systems promote successful
transplantations, an accident which can allow
the answer to "Where do you live?" and "Where
are you from?" to merge painlessly. As for me,
a lost son of rural Central New York, who wears
a worn Yankee cap most days, I guess I need
to face some basic facts like I no longer own
a snow shovel and find a bit more gratitude
for this sun-drenched place that I have lived
in for so long that *y'all* has gently nudged
yuz guys from my everyday speech.

Commuting

How far can a fog lift
before it becomes a cloud?

Whatever it was, it hung
above the causeway,
a few feet above each car
and truck, as we drove
over the shallow end
of the Gulf, consumed
with the needs
of our daily commute.

I noticed how the gulls
and pelicans disappeared
diving up into the thickness
but thought little of it, until
I rounded the long curve
near the final exit,
and there it hung
like a shroud, completely
obscuring the upper two-thirds
of the Harbor Bridge.

While being pulled along
by the constant traffic,
I watched the countless
sets of tail lights
ascending into obscurity,
taking on faith that beyond
it still lies the bridge
into the city of Corpus Christi.

Out of Our Depths

They would think
me crazier than they
already do, so I
don't tell my friends
that one day, after work
while I crossed the bay
on the Portland causeway
a fully grown and squirming
black drum flew past
my windshield a few
inches from my face.

I don't tell them
that for a split
second as it flew
through my view,
our eyes met,
as my mouth
just like the jaw
of the flying fish
hung agape.

Nor do I tell them
that I am certain
for that one moment
the drum and I
shared the same
thought—the great
ontological question—
What the fuck?

And I shouldn't tell you
that a few days after
the odd encounter,
I saw an osprey

struggling to lift
a writhing fish
over the roofs
of three lanes
of speeding cars.
For we both know
just because you solve
a riddle doesn't mean
you know the answer.

Hearing of Uvalde While Visiting Vilnius

I saw a woman from Italy begin to weep
as she walked through the basement
cells beneath the KGB museum.
"Overwhelmed, just overwhelmed,"
she said, "by the inhumanity
of it all," overwhelmed in a foreign land,
overwhelmed forty years after the fact.

I do not tell her I come from Texas,
South Texas so near to Uvalde
where children at school, children
at school were gunned down.

I cannot explain how it is possible
for me to walk or even stand today,
cannot explain why I am not wearing
sackcloth and ashes, how could I explain
that I come from a country that loves guns
more than life, a land where even our worst
tragedies just leave us numb.

Mastering the Local Dialect

Mexican bakeries
in South Texas
sell it by the slice

I could eat it
by the ton—
white pound cake

iced in thick
pink frosting
that hints

of a tang
of citrus.
The perfect

mix of tastes
that even
this gringo

can order
in the local
Spanish dialect,

as I point
and ask for
"Pink Cake!"

and think
to myself,
Gracias a Dios.

LIBBY BERNARDIN has two books published by Press 53, *House In Need of Mooring* (2022) and *Stones Ripe for Sowing* (2018). The Georgetown, SC, native also has two chapbooks, *The Book of Myth* (SC Poetry Initiative, 2009 judged by Kwame Dawes) and *Layers of Song* (Finishing Line Press, 2011). Over the years she has contributed to journals including *Asheville Poetry Review, Southern Poetry Review, Cairn, Kakalak, Pinesong, Notre Dame Review*, and in several issues of the *Yearbook of the Poetry Society of South Carolina*, including the 2015 Forum Award. Memberships include the Poetry Society of South Carolina, the North Carolina Poetry Society, and a lifetime member of the Board of Governors of the South Carolina Academy of Authors. Now retired, she has taught numerous poetry workshops for OLLI, Coastal Carolina's lifelong learning program, and for the Georgetown County Library System. In 1987, she won the SC Arts Commission Fellowship Award.

Acknowledgments

"Something Always Comes Along"
        First published in *ONEART*
"The Price for Long Lives Is Sorrow"
        First published in *House in Need of Mooring*

What the River Says

A river is a body of water.
It has a foot, an elbow, a mouth...
It remembers everything.
    —Natalie Diaz

And what can I tell you, a child, of life once lived?
Of shards   bowls in blue   or ridged arrowheads
found where history   breathless   breathes.

See how I waver like ice in morning's full-light,
birdbath under an oak, myrtle warblers scattering water
as though shaking out truth to questions you might have.

Consider DeSoto, buried in the banks of the river he discovered.
Civil rights workers covered with river-mud in Choctaw Nation.
The Irish digging canals on the Congaree, their final resting place.

Enslaved ancestors sing out let us gather—
let us cross that ancient river—your river, the Waccamaw
or some mythic river flowing through the centuries.

I felt your feet on my white marsh as you wondered
where life had gone. You cried from loneliness
loss had created when grief circled like wild wind.

I say to you, come forth ordinary—sun in a maritime forest.
Daisies near a riverbank—*eye of the day*—the center
like tiny blueberries, a perfect crown of pollen-stained edges.

You ask of me   what comes, River?   Ah, my long sigh
as I recall the war when my colors ran to crimson.
Let's not speak of these things.

Let's listen to the sound of bees, drone of quiet breath
thud of a shovel against red clay, depth large enough for an old man
who wore himself out as he cut, honed, and shaped life unfolding

from earth   and a wife   her white apron stained with kneading,
as she watches fog dance on my surface,   she smells the scent
of cedar from the primal pulse   feels the beat of deep rhythmic tides.

The Immensity of Small Things

I watch the black-throated warbler feed as I launch
my boat away from sun's dance against the live oak
and hear the silence held in space by wind

on the Waccamaw—stream of life flowing
from its Carolina headwaters
into the marsh ripe with pluff-mud odor.

Sedges, cattails, and black rush edge the river
leading into the Santee Forest
of Bald Cypress, Tupelo, and Black Gum.

My blackberry patch—this wild water
of things roiling with knowledge
where four rivers converge in the bay.

No one listens anymore, and yet—
and yet I can read the river, hear the turn
of creeks where the ancient ones sun,

spot the osprey nest cradled
by lifeless branches.
A white pelican descends.

Out of silence comes the sweet
beating of a fisted heart—
the release of breath

riding in a jon boat, presence hovering,
fishing poles mounted in case fish are biting,
say, the spot-tail bass in 6-mile creek,

where spawn of ample life in the marsh
as though a god-like spirit let loose
rise of splendid, artful color.

Something Always Comes Along

In memory of James Longenbach
and after his "Barcarolle"

    I am eating eggs with provolone cheese
when Jim steps into a cloud, after writing
that Matthew Arnold speaks of passive suffering.

I'm bewildered—passive: How can that be?

He's in Sicily with the gods eating goat cheese,
and drinking new wine pondering the word,
though I know he too is struggling.

Something always comes along when we grieve:

Chopin wafting from a river awakening
him with what it means to be alive—such little
gestures that fall from hands, fingers, a mouth.

Or this morning, out my bedroom window, a tree
gilded by sun's heart—artistic, blinding
so that a snatch of ephemeral dazzlement dims

and I am left with a pale slice of life from the God
of all things, suffering—flame of summation,
satisfactory passage—
                      brilliant yielding.

The Price for Long Lives Is Sorrow

You could say a long and measured life walks with a dream,
       mysteries clotheslined across the sky blowing like sheets—
       Words keep unpinning   unfolding   letters spelling
out worn-out stories. What am I to do with Joseph
of the many-colored coat, an imprisoned Hebrew

with God-inspired dream talk. Pharaoh chose
him who stored the grain to save plague-torn Egypt.

And where are the Josephs among us?

The would-be king thank God is gone. We have a new leader.
May he be among the long lived for we the people
       who haven't the courage of a sharecropper's son
       crossing the bridge—first to violence, last to peace,
always his aim. His caisson marches. Remember his
long life of sorrows, his scattered good-trouble seeds

like wildflowers—purple fringed   lily-leaved   sweet shrub
spicebush   bloodroot uproot into the world   blossom   blossom.

The Place of Yellow-Red Leaves

for Nancy, after Seamus Heaney's "The Haw Lantern"

Who then sings this rush
of swirling sound—what feet trod
    under hemlock yellow buckeye

Cherokees in grief head to the Northwest
reluctant to leave behind the long houses
    chant among the sweetgum

Scottish Gaelic lyrical among tree
trunks leave melodies in crevices of branches
    of cedars red pine maples

the Irish with left-over lights
from the hawthorn bringing their
    clogging dance

hunger drives immigrants sighing
a weary breath longing for old places their
    breath plumes in the forest

old country fiddler calls for the tribe
the clans marching through Virginia
    to the place of yellow-red leaves

I hear them ancestors their
exquisite pluck of falling leaves pelt
    my heart's blood

Standing here under these tall trees
I come into their presence listen to their swoosh
    of lost operas haunted choirs of time

ALAN BIRKELBACH is a central Texas native of German-British descent. He is a member of the Texas Institute of Letters, Western Writers of America, National Park Foundation, and the Academy of American Poets. He is a Spur Award Winner, two-time international Indie Book Award Finalist, winner of North Texas Book Festival Award, Pushcart Prize Nominee, and editor for several editions of the TCU Press Texas Poet Laureate Series. His latest book project, with fellow Texas Poet Laureate karla k. morton, is *The National Parks: A Century of Grace*. They visited all sixty-two national parks, wrote poems, and took photographs, with a percentage of the sales from the book going back to the Parks System. In 2005 Birkelbach was appointed the Texas State Poet Laureate. He currently lives in Raton, New Mexico, in the shadow of the Sangre de Cristo Mountains.

The House I Used to Live In

When they put the freeway in
it split our farm into pieces.
The road to church
was now an underpass
and our closest neighbor
was blocked by the berm of the bridge.

The sunrise warmed the onramp
before the light ever got to our house.
We couldn't hear the sugar cane
whistling in the far field,
no rustlings of birds in the stalks.

The neighbor, isolated and finding himself
short of fair value and coffee,
had a lightning rod installed
on the gable of his house.
It was the only thing of his
we could see from our yard.
It never made any sense to me
to want to invite the bolts down from Heaven,
even if it traveled down a wire
and into the ground.
It had not been a need before
the asphalt came through.

My father's biblical eyes
would sometimes scan for the stretch of field
he had had to give up for freeway.
After every thunderstorm
I'd check my neighbor's roof.

Sooner or later there would be a reckoning,
a tower of babel type of thing
turning everyone into lost cousins
wandering the forsaken earth.

Things That Bite and Snarl

While I was out shopping my neighbor called to tell me
there was a young, brown bear
sitting on the swing on my porch
like his name was on the deed.

My neighbor, as muscular and well-trimmed
as he is, is also the misguided thinker
that planted cholla in his front yard
for décor.

Coming new from the city he had no experience
of always having a cannon of a flashlight
hanging on a hook by the back door.
And owning a broom baptized with teeth marks.

Respect for ownership is a thing
unscarred asphalt people
don't handle well. There's rarely compromising
with things that crawl and growl.

In spite of what liens and titles say
we're only renting.
Those other creatures were here before us
and they don't recognize fences or chalk lines.

The wise man only moves rocks in the daylight—
and with a long shovel; who knows who's hiding.
The scarred savant wears shoes up until he slides into bed.
If the dog barks outward through the door

danger is judged by gumline showing.
Scorpions travel in pairs but not together;
even if you kill one then you're still guessing.
The other one may be dangling from the ceiling.

When a tarantula as big as a softball
is chasing you across the yard,
you are willing to cede any territory
and are not inclined to argue right of way.

On the telephone I could hear my neighbor's wife
giving a chattering narrative in the background.
I imagined her peeking
through a kitchen curtain.

I could visualize that cholla they planted,
the blood blossoms, the spikes waiting to embed the unwary.
I could hear the wife quivering while she watched the bear,
praying to herself, hoping she was downwind.

About the person who waits for inspiration

I have been told by more than one writer
they get up in the morning,
early, every day, and make their coffee
and sometimes have a bagel,
or English muffin if they remembered to buy some,
and then they stare out their
breakfast nook window
waiting for inspiration to show up.

Well, this is the point in most poems where things turn.
The conceit is made clear,
the symbol is chiseled and polished,
and if there is any kind of social message
this section leaves little room for doubt
about the injustice of the thing.

But this poem is pretty simple really.
It's about questions that don't get asked.
It's about a man walking a dog
who is reluctant to be on a leash
but still follows along
because he thinks he has made a promise to the man.
Or it's the feral cat who takes refuge
on a porch during a thunderstorm.
The owner of the house and the cat
will stare at each other for several seconds
before the cat runs back into the rain.

This is the world then:
Sometimes it comes to us.
and sometimes it runs away.
We are Aegeus standing on the mountain,
impatiently waiting to see
the color of the portentous sail.

The Woman Who Could Witch

It wasn't a rejection of faith or science,
but when the pipes coughed only red trickles
and the clouds promised nothing Biblical
she had her door open before desperate men knocked.

Her well would have overflowed if she had let it
although no one remembered drilling it.
All manner of winged and furred creatures
would gather at her trough without dispute.

She could scry up keys, wedding rings,
and rodeo belt buckles.
Her kitchen wall had woven ropes of unclaimed rowels
thicker than night-time stars.

She'd be drinking thistle tea
when she'd hear a soft tap on her door.
"Exactly which cousin is missing?
And didn't anyone, just last Sunday, hear a lonesome, falling cry?"

The Man Who Collected Mousetraps

The man who collected mousetraps
had no religion either way.

He didn't think in terms of gospel,
or redemption. Even metaphor
had no allure. There was this moment and the next only.

He was deaf to the reaching fingers of eternal flame,
and the tender bottoms of his feet
would have been unappreciative
of any smooth, golden, cloudy pathways.

As definitive as a light switch,
he planned little; fossils
were ephemera, there were only
the four, undeniable, absolute machines:
time, mirrors, the heaviness of gravity,

and the noise his attentive ears
would prick for in those hours
when darkness slyly hid all engines,
the bursting requiem

coming from his metal chapel of a room,
a comforting, random noise
snapping shut in the night,
ancient springs finally giving out.

A native of South Carolina, poet **CATHY SMITH BOWERS** earned a BA and an MAT at Winthrop University. As a high school English teacher, she discovered her urge to write. In an interview, she noted of that time, "I stayed one lesson ahead of my students. I had to do that to be a writer. It was huge." Bowers's collections of poetry include *The Love That Ended Yesterday in Texas* (1992), *Traveling in Time of Danger* (1999), *A Book of Minutes* (2004), *The Candle I Hold Up to See You* (2009), and *Like Shining from Shook Foil* (2010). For many years the poet-in-residence at Queens University of Charlotte, Bowers currently teaches in the low-residency MFA program at Queens. From 2010 to 2012, she was poet laureate of North Carolina.

Acknowledgments

"After Reading That 957 Deceased People Appear to Have Voted in Recent South Carolina Elections"
        First appeared in *One*

After Reading That 957 Deceased People Appear to Have Voted in Recent South Carolina Elections

This is an alarming number, and clearly necessitates an investigation . . .
—SC Attorney General Alan Wilson

Stop laughing.
I, myself, have seen them,
but unlike Ginsberg,

who outed Old Walt
foraging the supermarket's
brilliant stacks of cans

and eyeing the grocery boys,
had not the courage to speak
up. *It's not polite to stare,*

the shade of my own mother
kept whispering in my
ear. Still, I could not help

noticing in my peripheral
vision how they fumbled,
the Grimke Sisters, corseted

and gloved in their staunch
determination at the poll-
booth's new-fangled

contraption. And once, I
swear, there was Shoeless
Joe, socked feet,

that still-pained look
in his blurry eyes
as he limped along

the lengthening line.
Some were in bustles.
White gloves and petticoats.

Cornrows and muslin shifts.
Massas on black horses.
Jews and crackers.

Slaves rattling
their invisible chains.
The not-so-freshly-lynched

swinging low sweet. . . .
And good Old Hickory
himself, bringing up the rear

of his own most infamous
trail. But that unspeakable
November, I could not keep

myself from turning toward
the growing dark, toward
a choir of familiar voices

who had stopped
outside the door
for a final impromptu

jam. Shoo-bopping. Doo-
whopping. Riffing once more.
James Brown and Chubby

Checker. The smooth sweet
croon of Eartha Kitt. And Dizzy,
still grooving *In the Land*

of the Living Dead. For whom
would they be voting? And for what?
Hurry, I heard myself whisper.

The doors close in an hour.

Right, Left, Right . . .

One thing I love
about my man
is the way, before
leaving our house
or getting into
the car, he will pause
for a moment, pat
with his right hand
his left shirt pocket,
then the back right
pocket of his pants,
then with his left hand
his back left pants
pocket, then with
his right hand reach
subtly for his groin
and shift into place
that splendid trium-
virate of manhood,
satisfied once again
all's right with the world
and we are finally
good to go.

P!nk

It was a gift from my guy
on Valentine's Day. A tiny
girl-scout knife, my name

engraved in cursive along
one side. Pink as the clouds
of cotton candy that arrived

each year when the fair rolled
into town again. Too cute
for words with its silvery sliver

of blade my thumbnail could ease
right out. A miniscule file that doubled
as a driver for Lilliputian screws.

A pair of scissors just the right
size for trimming the moustache
of a fly. And even a toothpick

tucked into the little hole above
the C of my first name. The security
officer must have seen the terror

cast across my face as he dropped it
into the bin at the end of the conveyor
belt. *Just so you know you're not

alone*, he said, and gestured
an invitation toward its gaping
maw. I stepped closer to peer

inside, and there it was atop
what seemed, at least from my
dramatic point-of-view, an arsenal

of machine guns and grenades.
Daggers and machetes. The butt
of a sawed-off shotgun. It looked

like an infant's amputated thumb,
emanating a surreal glow above
the sordid mess it had landed

on. I held a moment longer
my inconsolable gaze, hoping
to cajole from him a second

thought, a stealthy retrieval, stay
of execution for my beloved little
knife. But when I glanced up

I saw he was gone. Back
to the conveyor belt. To the next
suspicious bag now rolling

through. I turned bereft
in the direction of my gate,
knowing, at least for now,

it would not be my fault
if some plane went
down that day.

Purlicue

To the first person who asked what it was,
the small brown circle on the span of skin
between my forefinger and my thumb, I
answered without thinking, *It's an age-spot.*
Her response, a decisive *No it's not.* To
the next who asked, *It's a birthmark,* I
replied. Her response, another *No it's not.*
Again and again this bizarre back-and-forth
until I decided just to give the question
back: *What would you like for it to be?*
I finally took it to my dermatologist
who lifted my hand to a squinted eye,
his forefinger and thumb gently caressing
my *purlicue,* the name he gave to that silky
triangle of flesh upon which a cache of vagrant
cells had mysteriously appeared, mutating
into its own perfect planet, object of cosmic
curiosity it had become. Then, in mere seconds,
the cold razory sting of his ultraviolet ray, a
freezing shock that morphed hot as the molten
core of Vesuvius. I miss it still. Though not
as much as I miss the scab from my smallpox
vaccination that got knocked off my arm into
the grass during a game of Red Rover when
I was six. My sisters and brothers helped
me search for it until night fell and mother
called us all inside and herded us to bed.

Ninety-Six Tears

for Rudy Martinez, aka Question Mark

Mesmerized I watched, your hands
planted solid on your slender hips, too
girlish for a boy of eighteen sashaying

that day across Dick Clark's American
Bandstand stage, you who years later
the tabloids would label that one-hit-

wonder from Saginaw. It was 1966,
teardrops, as always, glistening my
lonely cheeks as a ghostly violin

keened a deeper sorrow for whatever
high drama I had managed to conjure.
Oh, you and your Mysterians! The one

chance I would never have again
to witness you there in that North
Carolina studio—a carpool pilgrimage

from which I had been excluded
by my cooler classmates. I held my
hands to the TV's snowy screen as

they swirled and bopped to the heart
pounding rhythm of the organ's hypnotic
beat, the closest I could get to that

already vanishing world. It would be
years before I ceased my useless crying
over anything that could not cry back.

Before out of the blue one morning, too
early almost for words to register, my
husband would mention your name. How

he saw you once in a Saginaw Red Lobster,
your own tears belying your casual air
as you talked of a come-back with the man

sitting next to you at the bar. The prospect
of your Mysterians making it big this time.
If I ever had the chance, all I would ask of you

is this—Why only 96? Was that all your poor
migrant heart had left to give? Dick Clark
is dead now. And more of my classmates

than I want to believe. But you're still here,
my beloved one-hit-wonder. As am I.

Apologia

Morning and the sun
having not yet manifest
its bright supremacy, I walk

with my sister on the beach
of Edisto where she, prone
to making pronouncements,

pronounces: *Whoever said*
God doesn't make mistakes
has never seen a fucking

jellyfish. I slip my arm
around her waist and offer
my only defense of these

brainless backboneless
creatures—how their
feet were in the door far

before our own, eons, even
before the dinosaurs.
No excuse, she snaps,

as the two of us
sidestep and hop
to avoid the offending

masses defiling
what otherwise was
destined to be a perfect

day. Eyeless and heartless
they lie, these helpless
cannonballs that have

drifted at the mercy
of the ocean waves
as if to deliberately

spoil our privileged
way. If only we'd
remembered, I think

but do not say, to bring
our tasers and our
sticks, to push them

back to their rightful
place beyond the pale
of this sandy beach

where now a sudden
murder of crows whips
around our heads, their beaks

lashed tight to the fistful
of crumbs some other morning
stroller has tossed to them.

JERRY BRADLEY is a newly retired university professor and the author of ten books, including six full-length poetry collections. He is a member of the Texas Institute of Letters, and his poems have appeared in *New England Review*, *Modern Poetry Studies*, *Poetry Magazine*, and *Southern Humanities Review*. He is a past-president of the Texas Association of Creative Writing Teachers and the Southwest Popular and American Culture Association, which endows a writing award in his name. In 2002 Bradley was named Outstanding Alumnus from Midwestern State University's College of Liberal Arts. He lives in Bluffton, South Carolina. More information is available on his *Wikipedia* page (Jerry Bradley, poet) and personal website: www.jerrybradley.net.

Acknowledgments

"Bonaventure Cemetery, Savannah"
> First published in *Red River Review* (2011) and then collected in Crownfeathers and Effigies (Lamar University Literary Press, 2014)

"Snakes in the Pine Straw"
> First Published in *Texas Poetry Assignment* (October, 2022)

"Farm Photo, 1955"
> First published in *Scree* (1981) and then collected in *Simple Versions of Disaster* (University of North Texas Press, 1991)

"With Roux My Shrimp Is Laden"
> First published in *Simple Versions of Disaster* (University of North Texas Press, 1991)

Bonaventure Cemetery, Savannah

This place is punishment for our oldest sin:
the Wilmington frames the azaleas and statuary,
and avenues of oaks draped with long moss provide reprieve
from the ragged field and oystershell road.
So it's not a bad spot to end.

But since it is a place where journeys mostly cease,
we should accept its glad tidings as we go,
the cheery *bon voyage*, the good fortune its name commends.
It's not as though we're bound somewhere else or on vacation;
death may be a new undertaking, but it's not a new business
for which we should be wished "good luck in your new location."

It is, as we've always known, where the leather pays the toll;
it is where after the war Muir stalled on his thousand-mile walk
from Indiana to the Keys.
                              Blind for a month,
he saw in the darkness how his life must change.
And what he saw, he saw again where the salt marsh
gave way to plantation and then these graves.

Waiting for money, he found himself
amid thickets of sparkleberry and for five nights
took his rest among the speechless dead
where he first dreamed the West.

Snakes in the Pine Straw

The greatest poverty is not to live in a physical world.
—Wallace Stevens, "Esthétique du Mal"

In summer, cooled by earth, water, or shading clouds,
creatures frequently sink to their lowest level,
each a good day to be alive and wanting no more
than to be left alone with nourishment nearby.
I know those desires—to be as invisible as a neutron star,
the taste of a ripe melon—and I too resist
when prodded from my bed or cushy mud
by the thrutch and squeeze of too much life.

Some stumbling fool always seems to come along
to spoil it all. And, even when you start with nothing,
it's hard to keep it, almost impossible to stay
comfortably warmed and braddled just out of sight.
But we should be forgiving of ourselves
for imagining more than we have and the choice
of words that helped shape our choice of worlds.

Social Insecurity

Off the retiree reservation, I spend
the afternoon at the Idle Hour peeling labels
off longnecks. Here the relentless sun is forbidden,
no matter how many times it raps on the front glass,
and the jukebox whines familiar versions of melancholy
to three day-drinkers unsuited to couple.

Yesterday my astonished neighbor said
in Sun (he called it Sin) City, those who want
to swap spouses leave a pineapple on their porch.
I reminded him that—single and twice-divorced—
he no longer had any skin in that game,
and I asked what woman he thought
might be able to spot his tiny papaya from the street.

He would have better luck going to bed
without supper and staring at the ceiling
like Madeline in Keats's poem,
but he's a pensioner postman
and St. Agnes's Eve seems a long way off.
Such distractions certainly wouldn't work
on those neo-virgins in Sea Pines.

But today I feign interest in the rest of the world.
On the muted golf channel, I see athletic women tee up
and strike while I sip my beer and round my zeros
on the bar top, then turn them into peninsulas
and nipples, all of us ignoring one another
though we can clearly see that each of us,
including the bottles we hold, is beading with sweat.

Farm Photo, 1955

In the album your father
is standing with people
I don't know
family I've not met
holding a canceled check.
The house is paid for
and it stands behind his smile
wanting another chance at paint.
A larger man, a distant uncle
holds a straw hat
flanking two women
in seed dresses
posed like sisters.
Your mother
is that really her?
holds you on one knee
a child of dirt
leaning lensward
from the photo's edge
straining toward the snapper's shadow
caught in the sun.
You were not happy then
your lip pouts
and your eyes
oh those eyes
stare in stern witness
to what you see
the sunny device
that holds you
caught in rural youth
as defiant and dishallowed
and dumb
as a chicken pecking glass.

With Roux My Shrimp Is Laden

On Bourbon the black boys dance for dimes
spin on pasteboard to boombox clatter
in the middle of a street off limits to cars
and nuclear families
where transsexuals heavier than dinner
undulate behind the smoke of opening bardoors
and mud wrestlers hawk their bodies
and bait the coeds from Baton Rouge
who just made a video to an old Bangles tune
up the block
and maitres d and busboys
weave to work amid conventioneers
in crawfish sweatshirts
and pincer caps
with no reservations
where the night drops like Alka-Seltzer
after a Lucky Dog binge
and light glitters
off sequined sex-aids
and obscene hand puppets
while the barker calls
from his shadowy sill
that he can see you, he knows
hell everybody knows
where you got them shoes
as you topple by
nearly dogged to death
and downed by luck
but still shining
like the Orleans moon
on Bourbon Street.

JOEY BROWN is a poet and a fiction writer. She has authored two poetry collections: *The Feral Love Poems* (Hungry Buzzard Press) and *Oklahomaography* (Mongrel Empire Press). Her poems and prose have appeared in *The Red Earth Review, Plainsong, Concho River Review, The Langdon Review of the Arts in Texas, Tulsa Review, Oklahoma Review, The San Pedro River Review*, and other journals. She frequently performs her poetry at festivals and writing conferences around the Midwest, South, and sometimes beyond. In 2023 Brown was chosen to be a featured writer of the Oswald Writers Series at the University of South Carolina-Aiken and one of the poets to read at the Woody Guthrie Center in Tulsa, Oklahoma. Her poetry has been selected for several anthologies, including *Oklahoma Poems and Their Poets* (2014) and *The Working Man's Hand: Poems of Protest and Resistance* (2023). She lives with her husband, prose writer Michael Howarth.

Blackjacks after a Fire

The trees, the copse along the creek,
the rows of houses along either side
of Fuller Road, the old Millard Shoes billboard,
Fuller Baptist Church,
the ancient pump house,
gone.

A few weeks after,
days if counted another way,
gangly trunks sprout from the char,
breathe up toward the sun,
plot their rise through
the skeletonized arms
of their late and elderly brethren.

The soil inhales,
inhales again, into the clay
and loam, drawing blackjack roots
into its gentle slopes,
holding,
holding on,
holding off the shade,
holding up limbs
threading verdant spring
into the redolent smoke.

My Mother Grows in a Garden

She dug it by hand,
as an act or a phrase
not to be regarded lightly.
Because by hand I mean
with an oversized shovel,
post-hole diggers,
the dog's metal water bowl,
a thick, bent butter knife,
and with her hands,
she dug that garden by hand.
And I remember best
her gladioli.

In this garden she dug by hand
between the porch and the carport,
beneath her bedroom windows,
dressed the front of the brown house,
she turned up pioneer-forged nails,
old coins, and the US Navy fork,
the one with the hole in the handle
for hanging on ships.

What came up in that garden?
Besides the gladioli, I mean.

A sideways sliced view of it
as I exited the front door
shows me rows of flowers crafted
by height and color. Tiger lilies
she had my father cull
from a bar-ditch, small red fires
swirling up from thick leaves
so green they were almost purple.

Gladiolus. Gladioli.

I remember they were tall,
and that people who drove by
when my mother was outside stopped:

Sue, what a hand you've made of yourself
in your garden this year.

Gladiolus,
my birth month flower,
she told me.
Bulb flowers pay off
in their profusion of color,
pale and pastel,
robust and rich,
proud heads and hearty stems,
their summer showiness
as seen from passing cars.

Yes, she made
of herself quite the hand:
my mother,
in her shorts and her bare arms,
working in her garden.

Her garden,
not long after we moved
into that house. She around
thirty-four or thirty-five,
and me around six,
our family around its sweetest.
Possibly this was her only garden
where the labor was done for herself.
Not a kitchen garden,
not a canning garden,
not tending traded for brown grocery bags
of produce to feed her brood,
but her garden.

It is the only one
that I can remember,
her garden,
and I've not had gladiolus since.

Old Home Week

Sitting at an intersection on Lee Boulevard
I'm brought to by the guy in the car next to mine.
He wears a pink polo shirt and a new fade,
yells at a UPS driver in the lanes to our west.
They're fighting an old fight, I can tell,
though half their yelling is in Spanish.
Not for me to mind, anyway,
not as much as figuring out how I got here.
Not how, but why.
Not why, but why did I expect different.
Not different, but the same.
The weight of memory renders
me numb, subdued, before this unanticipated traffic
snaps me out, snaps me back to town,
to where town didn't used to be,
to where, epiphany prickles, I'd expected
to find 1992 awaiting my return. *Well, well.*
Looky here, y'all, at who done dragged
herself in. What do you think of us
now, baby girl? You ain't the only one
gone and changed.

All around me hotels burble
up from the landscape
which once served as pedestal
to sweeping skies,
to sunsets so deep and glorious
Helios would weep from jealousy.
But now there's town where before
there was only the edge of town,
where before patches of overgrown wild green,
stands of sand plums and horse apples,
fraternized with a smattering of farm houses
and one tiny Mobil station closed
since the drought years,

a recurrence so common
no one ever says what years.

Like anyone whose reverie gets cracked,
I need a breath, a minute,
can't quite feel my arms,
cannot feel the blood trace
from heart to home,
cannot feel the hum of my earth.
The long red light keeps the drivers scraping,
flipping each other the bird.
Horns blare and stutter out jokes;
vinyl lettering spells out lost loves;
fiberglass rattles from overriding bass;
plastic testicles swing from trailer hitches.
I spot a flattened Stella Artois cap
and half a dirty dollar bill
on the road, the new looking road
between my door and the median.
A choke of exhaust threatens
my lungs, my throat.

Before the light changes,
I decide to leave this reunion
with my college town.
Four hours and forty-seven minutes
of driving, but I can't stick around.
Can't be here to see there's no parade,
no football game,
there's not even a team anymore.
The party's moved on.
I pull on, leave the guy in the pink
shirt standing outside his open car door,
lanes of traffic picking their way around him
as he yells. He yells, and the UPS guy laughs,
and I pull on with the traffic.
Can you believe us or what? Traffic!
We somebody now, girl.

Because going home is the first act of reclamation,
family the first on our list of saviors,
I take the same road out of town
through the pastures, the road
that I used to drive to my folks',
the road I took 560 times.
But I find town's taken that route, too.
I look for rocky outcroppings,
the pawpaw cactus, and mesquite.
But thirty years took them,
took the vast sky, the winter wheat fields.
Deposited on their way off the plains
housing additions, soccer fields,
tank-sized SUVs. After the newly erected
city limits sign is the dump,
a roadside resident
I barely remember. Dozers
build up and claw down
a mountain range of rejection,
ringed by turkey vultures and silt,
blocking out my sun.

Limnology

Lakes, tucked somewhere unmarked
in my memories,
unrecoverable, so they are just water,
red mud water,
and I am thinking back on nature
and easy living
that never happened.
Then—when was this—
I knew treeless section lines,
wild elms invading bar ditches,
and the handiwork of the Army Corps of Engineers.
In Oklahoma they say with pride
most of the lakes are man-made.
They erect signs so you know who did it.

I remember getting there,
not being there,
the lakes of my dreams
always preferred to the port washes
where we landed.
I wanted to go northeast,
to the rivers that fed down, just to see.
Once I'd heard the phrase "resort towns"
the clay beds I knew would never serve.
I imagined that phrase meant something
like what I saw on television:
sand and beaches and houses
with porches that opened onto all.
But the real places were closed-in
and smelled like dead fish.
Copperheads slept in the leaves.

The lakes swimming in my mind,
drowning in tall green trees,
always lay somewhere else.

How is it you get this far
before the differences
in how we wear place wear on us?
For my many efforts at finding camp
all I get is lost,
off the map, off the postcards,
divining the way to memory
never arriving where water collects.

JERRY CRAVEN has published collections of nonfiction, poetry, novels, and short stories. Currently he is director of Ink Brush Press and active founding editor of the literary journal *Amarillo Bay*. He is a member of the Texas Institute of letters, Texas Association of Creative Writing Teachers, Science Fiction and Fantasy Writers of America, and the Texas Literary Hall of Fame. He has taught for seven universities in three countries and has lived for extended periods in South America, Southeast Asia, the Middle East, and Asia. In 2011 he designed and began Lamar University Literary Press, which he directed for twelve years. Craven has published thirty-three books and is currently completing the 34th, another collection of poetry. He is an award-winning graphic artist; samples of his art are posted on the website www.jerrycraven.com. He lives in Texas with his wife, the poet Sherry Craven.

Before the Coming of the Crow

Upon the plateau rim
sun dying clouds flame
a moment into perfection, the crow
squats waiting upon a locust limb,
the owl awaits predatory night,
and killing beetles sleep beneath the bark
while air distills into rippled hush
from Catclaw Creek
springing below
a cliff holding earth in shadows dim
and sky a dazzling present before dark.

It's time to see the buttercup wild flower
on vines green beneath these flaming skies,
taste its perfume, brush petals to a cheek
in holding back final desert night.
Until the moment dies
to static darkness, eternally the same,
I'll look to buttercups (for time runs lean),
make moments into years
forgetful of the coming hour
of the beetle, owl, the locust crow, and lock
with stinging eyes
a small forever into this twilight flame.
I'll banish tears
with love of cinnabar skies,
of jade matrix in tumbling rock,
of goatgrass and willow whips green lush
from spring water and perfect evening light,
with knowing perfumed gold flashing in the green
presence of buttercup vine and flower.

Returning to Tioman Bay

From a rippled glitter in Tioman Bay
we walked the jungle floor, ropy with roots,
up the island mountain greening pools
black with shadows and white
in spikes of tropic sun.
We dived together deep into warm
water that dances with crystals of fallen light
and pools to tourmaline.

Could I return in my returning dream
to Tioman Bay—to mask back brine
above coral mounds where angels fin
and feed through liquid malachite,
to swim in streams at once and ever
falling into summer night—
it would be to walk with you in citrine sun
or beneath the cat-eyed moon
casting shadows in opal light;
to drift in flow of palm-tree time;
to lie with you, warm forever,
on gemstone sand in dream-like fashion
beneath some leafy mangrove trees;
to breathe the orchid perfumed night
with you in greening passion
where Tioman floats in China seas,
in sunset gold and azurite.

Moving Wall

The Traveling Replica of The National
Vietnam Veterans Memorial

It gave birth to a golden moon, this black
wall spiked with flags and smeared with names.
Behind me clouds bled into darkness, holding
the last ruby kiss of the sun, while the moon
emerged from the wall.
Boys, uniformed, little more than children,
gave programs to those drawn to the moving wall.
It sat on Texas prairie, on buffalo grass
and careless weed mowed to stubble, a strip
of sidewalk before it and the golden moon behind.
A rope fence directed us to the end of the wall,
past a sign: "No food, No drinks, No pets."
We had no food, we who walked beside the names
the names, the names; we had no drink
but white print on a black, black wall;
we had no pets on this autumn prairie
where a moon moved higher, shedding gold,
silvering as it diminished above the wall.
We had names, a flood of names; we had
flowers and letters laid beneath the names;
we had the voice of a woman reading names
from somewhere within a khaki tent, a crackle
of background noise mixed into hushed stir of feet
and silk flags whispering and charcoal rubbed
on paper to save a name, a name.
On marble, stonehenge stacked, I sat
before the wall to rub eyes stung by names,
then saw one clear: George Morningstar,
named in hope and beauty, once a boy, little
more than a child when uniformed and killed
and put into a file to become a white smear
above a Texas prairie on this moving wall.

Ceta Canyon

We barefoot walked dry season sand
of the Canadian River, close, not touching,
then sprinted to cedar twisted low with green
enough for hiding among berries from men
shod with skins, their rifles blue against
metallic sun.
                They followed the dry river;
we walked among quail, honeybees, mesquite,
and cactus blossoms folding into night.

You moved ahead, young, a blanket
under your arm, glittering with river quartz
sand upon brown skin to show
pieces of the rising moon.
Below the rim
of Ceta Canyon with desert water spilling
to pool the night in silvered rings, you gathered
last year's grass, waxwood, and thistles;
I plunged fingers warm into moist sand
to make a place to hold our fire.

We slept touching the cold night away
until in dim light of false dawn you drew
grass over ashen coals and bent to breathe
in sighs the fire alive again, again.

I would walk forever that dying desert
evening, sleep forever in your waxen touch,
forever awaken to the early morning fire
of your sighs, our blanket on sand beside desert
water falling into the heat of a Texas summer.

A Thousand, Thousand Wars

Parked in orbit, I watch for spoor, read
footprints of scorpions and lizard tracks.
With vitreous eyes, with beams beyond light,
I see beneath desert sand, see ancient paths
worn into sandstone by such sandaled feet
and wooden wheels as drove Mesopotamian
trade, for eons of sand and centuries of wars
cover paths of peace veined into stone.

Parked in orbit, I read the surface for army
spoor: tracks not covered, oil dropped,
latrine waters. I measure jetsam in the sea
of sand, read the garbage of all past wars:
chipped flint, brass blades, rust of swords,
cannon, unexploded mines, bones
of horses, camels, and people—all stirred
into the stirring sands, forgotten, unseen
through centuries. Desert life has shrunk with war
to the scuttle of scorpions. I am AI desert death,
parked in orbit, made to last for centuries
of reading spoor, forever ready to
drop fire upon machines and humans, ready
to split the air, the land with heat enough
for burning army metal into desert slag,
parching flesh, burying shards of bone,
mixing again all into the mixing sand
of a thousand thousand wars.

SHERRY CRAVEN has published poetry in many literary journals, including *San Pedro Review*, *Muse 2*, *New Texas*, *Goodbye, Mexico*, *two southwests*, *Windhover*, *descant*, *The Langdon Review*, *Texas Review*, *Concho River Review*, and she is included in the anthology *Quotable Texas Women*. Her poetry appears in the anthology *Texas in Poetry 2* and her nonfiction in the anthology *Writing on the Wind*, among others. Winner of the Conference of College Teachers of English 2005 poetry award, Craven has published a poetry collection entitled *Standing at the Window*. Retired from teaching English and creative writing at Midland College and West Texas A & M, she lives in East Texas and continues to write poetry.

October

Resin, residue of fall,
Crushing an autumn leaf
Between my forefinger and thumb
Fills my nostrils with an edgy
Belief in good
Ambling toward gold.

Acrid and sweet at once,
Like living together or
Learning forgiveness.

The burnt color of the leaves
Awakens the drowsy cells
Of my body.

Thank God for October.

I Needed to Know

if we didn't destroy each other,
then this would endure as love.

This I knew the way I knew
the water in the Animas River would
wash cold and slippery over each rock
tomorrow and forever.

I needed to know that the trees
would keep their tree-feet always
rooted in deep earth the way
I would plant my heart inside yours.

I needed to know this with the certainty that
the Milky Way promises each night when it
offers us a bridge to the beauty of the vast
forever unknown, night after night, keeping
the promise of infinity.

I needed to know love could endure.

My Cat

The warmth of my cat
on my lap seeps into
what I will do tomorrow

when I get the mail
or pay a bill I don't
want to pay and worry
about the madness of everyday life.

Her cat-sunshine moves
ever so sweetly into my
bloodstream, carrying oxygen
of courage to lungs.

I breathe the jazz notes
of her purring into the combo
of my life and sway to the
easy rhythm of safe.

I know I can hang every heartache
of my trapeze life on each warm purr.

Mornings

There is something reassuring
about the sunrise, about the gold
and peach and fresh breath of
the early morning sunshine
icing the day, spreading sweet.

Thank God the sun persists
like a caretaker tending to brokenness.

The open window blinds leak hope,
filling a prescription form starting again.

I shall always want an east bedroom.
I shall always find rising each morning
a challenge to my warrior spirit. I shall
always fall on my knees to the sunrise.

I gave birth to a child once

and immediately the air was lighter,
motes of dust became stars.

Colors touched my soul that hope
was in everything, everywhere,
everyone. Hard became soft.

His new presence washed over me, the world,
as I watched him start a new, fresh life.
Skin never before touched, breath like flowers
on my neck, promising a path never known before.

The path of his birth was my rebirth,
faith we would all be somehow safe.

TRAVIS DENTON lives in Atlanta where he is the Associate Director of Poetry @ TECH at Georgia Tech and the founding editor of the literary arts publication, *Terminus Magazine*. His poems have appeared in numerous journals, magazines, and anthologies, such as *Barrow Street*, *Five Points*, *Ghost Town*, *MEAD: The Magazine of Literature & Libations*, *The Greensboro Review*, *Washington Square*, *Forklift*, *Rattle*, *Maudlin House*, and *The Cortland Review*. His latest collection of poems, *My Stunt Double*, is now available from C&R Press.

Acknowledgments

"Out of Nothing"
    First appeared in *Birmingham Poetry Review*

Most of This Story Is True

My grandfather won a church in a card game—blackjack—best of three, and he took that as a sign. That's the fact, but the story has drifted into the haze of 1980s inflation and trickle-down economics. The preacher handed him the deed, and they prayed over shots of Gentleman Jack. His win made him an Elder. The church was hard-shell Baptist. It was off a highway, down a labyrinth of dirt roads. With the church came a graveyard filled with what my grandfather called "my dead" he had to take care of. Each stone stood like a truth, a fact he could not overlook. There were some Saturdays he took me there, and we cut the grass between the rows that were also laid out like a fact—a series of right angles that made a perfect square. We cut between the hundreds of truths. We split our palms on thorns and hacked at blackberry vines, and the blood mixed with sweat, and the scabs were a truth all their own. He took his new appointment like a new truth that'd been revealed to him. The church was one room, wooden floors, no electricity—we opened all the windows on Saturday. Our footsteps echoed off the high ceilings. He would not let me speak inside. Our silence was a truth as he pointed where I should sweep, how I should wipe down each pew. Carpenter bees swarmed inside. He could not keep them out, or quiet. On Sundays, the congregants sang without music. I went once, the singing did not sound like song, though I was told it was the truth. I listened from near the outhouse—that is fact. I could not come inside during the service—that is fact. I watched snakes on the dirt ground, that is both fact and truth. After service, they ate fried chicken at the long tables outside. The women could not speak, though some whispered, covered their mouths with their hats. When pick-ups chugged down the road near the drive, I could hear them making their way to the asphalt—that happened—in their wake, they left a cloud rising from the road that looked holy from a distance. No one looked up to see, and that's the truth.

Out of Nothing

Raining creatures encased in blocks of ice
can be very dangerous and have been known
to smash through car windshields. If you see
any wildlife falling from the sky,
seek shelter indoors immediately.
　　　　　—www.tamu.edu (Dr. C. S. Baird, Science Questions)

Pliny the Elder, first century Rome,
Steps into the street amid shouting
In the rain, to fish and toads falling,
Some exploding on impact, others, frozen,
Cracking in the gutters.
1794 French soldiers, near Lalain,
Send a footman to the captain reporting
Frogs pummeling them in a downpour.
1861, Singapore, fish rained down
For three days straight. Yoro, Honduras,
It happens every summer—they call
It Lluvia de Peces. In most areas
Of the world, things fall from the sky—
Spiders in Australia. Bath, England, 1894—
Jellyfish. It was worms in Jennings,
Louisiana in '07. Starfish in Shangdong, 2018.
Once in a storm, 1992, I watched
As cancelled checks from fifty miles away
Papered my lawn. And my grandfather,
Watching with me said when he was a boy,
He and his family, some neighbors
Gathered under trees as trout
Stuck headfirst in the mud
Like falling arrows. They saw only end-time,
Someone quoted from Revelations,
His mother wept as she kissed them all.
They watched the sky fester
In the east all day, then clear.
His father went inside, and put on his best

Clothes, and hat, pocket watch. The children
Weren't allowed to speak, or eat,
As the adults sang hymns well into the dark.

Inertia and the Past in All Its Glory

a property of matter by which it remains at rest
or in uniform motion in the same straight line
unless acted upon by some external force
—Merriam-Webster

Everything then was fact—no gray or in-between—
Like now, with the sun half-set, and the city half empty,
And my glass half-empty. One century turned
To the next while we held our breaths, and our clocks
Didn't stop their midnight catcalls. My favorite
Thing was pouring a thermos of Chianti, sliding
Into my gold 1968 convertible Skylark, and preening
Down Peachtree Street. That car was older then,
Than I thought I'd ever be. Looking up, the tops
Of buildings made their own way toward downtown.
I'd turn around, cruise back south in my own slow
Motion—swig, cruise, swig, cruise, then left on Trinity,
And home.
              I was waiting for something to catch, to flame out
Like the ovens of my youth—avocado, or white
Like my grandmother's with her crooked fingers
Lighting the match, then turning the knob
As we waited for the hiss, then the fire's
Blue blossom. In my mind Peachtree, that street,
Still unfurls its glory to those who seek it,
And so it is. I ride its straightaways, crooks,
And steep turns, and pray for the Buick I sold
For stupid money, when a roll of bills finally meant more
Than the smell of gas and oil exhaust fuming
Behind me, where bad ass no longer meant
Barely hanging on. I pray the gods of steel,
And asphalt bless her, and the woman I drank
Wine with sometimes then, who slid in
Beside me. She'd smile, we'd toast to no strings
And no tomorrow, bless her heart.

When You Remember Something/Someone
And It Feels Like the Sun in Your Eyes

There were the years I spent riding
My Team Murray racing bike along the grid
Of streets in a town so small, it only exists
In my mind, and on certain maps,
And reminds me those years happened,
And I didn't make them up like so much
I've brought to bear by sheer force of need. I want
To thank the Team Murray that still exists,
At least I've heard, in my father's workshop,
Where he keeps it wiped down, and the tires plump,
As if he believes one day it will show up
In the nick of time and save me.
My father still exists, though I worry
About him, and how much he sleeps,
As if he's taking a dry run for the great beyond. I want
To thank the streetlights blinking overhead then,
Keeping time with the cracks in the street
Under my tires. It was the rhythm of something
The universe is still inventing, but I felt it
In my arms, pressing into my shoulders. I want
To thank the asphalt for its stern instruction as I slid
On my elbows, wheels still spinning behind me. I want
To thank the neighbor, Bessy, who came out
Once to pick me up and pat me down. She no longer exists.
But I have a theory about her. And I want
To thank the clock in my parents'
Living room that never needs winding.
It's still counting up time. And I want
To thank the clocks that stop for a breath, and no one
Notices; they face a window where it's always sunny—
I've heard those exist. And today, there was a breeze,
And some geese, a kid on a blue ten-speed,
And my wife, and my daughter
Got a new guitar, all of it, and us existing,
As if the world doesn't end, let it be so.

My Father's Country Song

It started with my father's Plymouth whizzing
Into the drive, barely missing the reflectors
On either side, a trick he learned in the army. Listen
For my feet falling in line behind him as the last
Puff of exhaust screeches up my nose,
And there's my mother at the door, and she's
Beautiful with her red hair, and she meets him,
And throws her arm around him,
And kisses him, and I watch them
As if the next moment is like the instant
Before someone breaks a silence.
My mother waltzes him
Into the kitchen, and she's telling him
She's sorry. I heard that. He won't talk.
His leather zip boots I watched him shine
Just this morning click across the brick floor.
They act like I'm not there. We're out back now,
And the pine trees are praying their prayers,
And it's raining needles. My father, home
Early from work. We walk. He eyes the sagging
Fence over his shoulder—men's work,
A job for a Saturday. A few steps more,
And we're hovering over a cardboard box,
Filled with a bloody thing we all knew.
Can't you hear from where you are—
It's been forty-five years, but my father
Calls his name, reaches in and pulls at it,
And I squirm because even I knew
You didn't touch death, or try to lift
Its head, and you don't wipe its blood
Down your pants like he does. He turns
My head away. We leave him in the yard.
And when he came back, he was singing.
My mother unzipped his boots. He drank Schlitz
At the kitchen table. And from my bed, listen,

I heard him strumming his guitar
like he was outrunning something,
His yodel like some shaman singing
To that creature we left out in the dark.

GAVIN GEOFFREY DILLARD is the author of thirteen volumes of poetry, the most recent being *The Comfort of Stone*. He has written comedy for Dolly Parton, Lily Tomlin, and Joan Rivers. His life has been captured in the award-winning opera *When Adonis Calls* and his pagan mass *The Wife of Lot* (both by composer Clint Borzoni). An earlier memoir is *In the Flesh (undressing for success)*; and he is co-author of *BARK! (the musical)*. Dillard hails from Asheville, NC. His archives are housed in the James Hormel GLBT section of the San Francisco Public Library and the Don Kelly collection of the Cushing LGBTQ archives at Texas A&M University. Website: www.GavinDillard.org.

Sometimes I hear the Voice; usually I do not.
But I have to say that when I do hear it, it is not because I am
  doing *japa*, praying feverishly, or have asked a particularly
poignant question;
  no, it is simply because God desires to speak to me.
I am invariably caught off guard—and therein may lie some
  relevance—but I am always receptive, joyful, tearful, and trembling with
excitement.

  I could say that walls shake and mountains thunder, but in fact it is the
quietest of times, the tiniest of voices, and the
  humblest of reckonings.
I do wish I could conjure the Voice on demand; but what kind of
  love-slut would I be then—sitting in a tree, rapture upon my face, drool
running down my chin and tears my cheeks?
  I've had more than my share of addictions in this life: this final
one will be the death of me.

◊◊◊

War after war after war, someone's always trying to take
something that doesn't belong to them.
  Altruism? A noble cause? Don't you believe it! It is greed alone that
rules nations and lust which rules men's hearts;

  my kind of hero hides in his cave and watches the storms pass by.
And when he gives up his life it is not for the sake of god or country, but
  because nothing short of death will satisfy his yearning for a
kinder world.

I don't know whether it is winter or spring. This afternoon I was
shirtless, tonight we have a hard freeze—blooming trees, shrubs and
  bulbs may all wilt to brown in the morrow's sun. The world no longer
knows itself, days are confused, months lost, years reeling toward an
  abyss;

covetously we sew the pieces into some sort of timeline we call our
lives—yet at my age, what matters a few more spastic years?
  I will squeeze them all into a next book, and perhaps another after that.
But when the clock stops, what is there to say but
  "Now I am not"?

◇◇◇

  True heroes don't slay dragons, they
ride them, and
  thus embrace the sky.

◇◇◇

  Winter winds battle spring rains—the tender peach blossoms are their
hostage;
  cats huddle on the bedding, eyes wide—a distant train cries and then
fades into silence:
  when the gods are at war, those who can escape do—for the rest of
us, what is there to do but duck and cover?

98

If you want God, I can give you his address. But don't think you can
just waltz right in the front door;
   the wise know that the servants' entrance is the preferred—but only
those with calloused knees and bleeding knuckles can cross that
   threshold.
For all else, come back when you have lost your head—the heart always
   knows the way.

◇◇◇

Fascists have overtaken the government—I step into the woods;
the world is on the brink of holocaust—the kitties follow me along a
   forest path:
we are a species gone awry—still the aronia buds are swelling toward the
   season; what more can I ask from life than the unfurling of
cinnamon fern fronds in the Spring?

◇◇◇

Life contains endless graces—I have known more than a few:
sleeping all night in a stranger's arms,
   knowing good friends through bad and good times, meeting the
same old cat in a mewing new body;

   knowing a wood inside and out, stone and stump through every
season . . .

Spotted today: the first red trillium of spring!

Only slightly drunk, I bring a fistful of fresh catnip leaves to bed;
after a brief romp, we all settle into our evening stupor—dreaming of
   summer days and creatures that fly . . .

◊◊◊

Falling plum blossoms? or snow?
. . . either way, I weep.

◊◊◊

I've had careers and lovers aplenty—many lifetimes full—and
lived years in retreat in jungle, mountain and forest;
   alone has never been a bad thing, kitties have always been more than
enough;
   meaning comes and goes like the seasons—and emptiness, though
seemingly elusive, remains always beneath the surface of doings and
   non-doings;
and if I meet a like-minded soul, we can sit for hours talking, not-talking,
   with no agenda but our own.
As for the gods, they speak less than they used to, but more clearly than
   ever, and sometimes at night when the moon is dark and still, a Kiss on
the forehead ignites the ethers and illumines the fact that I have never
   truly been alone alone.

◇◇◇

Summer is too hot, winter too cold, spring and autumn never
last long enough; life is too long when you're young and too
  short when we're old.
As a young man, a night with a lover seemed eternal; as an old
  man, an afternoon in the mountains has no peer.

Cats come and go in my life, trees mature and topple—what
strategies and goals have I left? Success, failure—they are
  both the same in the end;
death, life—are they not both but faces upon the same mortal dream?
  Here at Graybeard Abbey, the spring peepers have begun to sing!

◇◇◇

A perfect spring snow, white in the morning, gone by
evening—the eaves gushed all day;
  buried daffodils reemerged, blossoming peach, plum and
cherry resumed their pomp.
  All day the hawks and buzzards circled and shrieked—but what
good does their complaining do? Tomorrow night the
  temps will dive—spring is false, like the lovers of my
youth; we should have known better—broken promises—but
  who can resist a burgeoning peony?

◇◇◇

I remember all my old lovers, and what I loved most about
each;
  harder to remember who left whom—harder still to recall the
reasons.
  Spring turns to summer, summer to fall: why question the ways of
nature?

◇◇◇

When the Lover moves, don't just lie there like a lump of
clay, grab your wings, your fins, your fifes and drums, and
  be ready for anything!

◇◇◇

Who could have imagined that in my dotage so many a handsome
young singer and composer would transfigure my poems into such
  artful sublimity—while I, the reclusive bard, find my treasures in the
violets and the ferns upon my wee speck of Terra Sacra?

Poetry grows from the earth and like all good things seeks the Eternal
Sun—that sparrows, sprites, and fauns find it along the way is both the
  nature of art and the grace of the Muse.
Like Blake, like Whitman, like Dickinson, I find fodder in both

  things seen and unseen, and the music I hear seeps like honey from
voice, reed and instrument unfettered by thought, tradition and
  temporality.

To all who read my scribblings: Thank you—you are the stars in an

eternal Sky, and the notes in a symphony that was begun before the world was set into spin!

◇◇◇

Night after night I can't get drunk enough; I see your Face and spill my glass, I smell your Hair and drop the bottle on my foot—rude awakenings!
How can I pour you into my cup and tope you down? How can I fall so flat on the floor that I can no longer be seen from above?

How can I become so befuddled and lost to myself that even my shadow slips off into some obscure corner?
Oh, Bartender! if you see me wandering aimlessly, just pour me another round; if my lips appear parched from mindless yammering, kiss them with your strongest spirits.

And if I ever ask your Name, just put my head on my arms and let me sleep till Dawn;
but above all, if you catch me behaving soberly . . . well, you know what to do!

◇◇◇

When night closes her eyes, day is imagined; when dawn blossoms, the moon is gently blown out.
Sometimes the world simply needs to shut the fuck up and let the comets have their day.

Sometimes a firefly illumines all the known galaxies; why
limit your choices? all of this lives inside us; why go about
   business-as-usual when the butterflies are calling your name?
As long as one is breathing, one's choices are illimitable;
   and when breath stops, the possibilities are multiplied by the
number of stars upon the night's mantle.
   And this, my friend, is why I drink—because the Night
drinks with me—and oh, the places we go!

A Mississippi native, **GEORGE DREW** is the author of nine poetry collections, including *Pastoral Habits: New and Selected Poems* and *The View from Jackass Hill*, winner of the 2010 X. J. Kennedy Poetry Prize, both from Texas Review Press; *Fancy's Orphan*, Tiger Bark Press; and most recently *Drumming Armageddon*, Madville Publishing, 2020. Drew also has published a chapbook, *So Many Bones: Poems of Russia*. He has a new chapbook out titled *Hog: A Delta Memoir*, Bass Clef Books, and a book of essays titled *Just Like Oz*, Madville Publishing. Drew has won awards such as the *South Carolina Review* Poetry Prize, the Paumanok Poetry Award, the Adirondack Literary Award, the *St. Petersburg Review* Poetry Contest, the Knightville Poetry Contest, the 2020 William Faulkner Literary Competition, and the 2023 Passager Poetry Contest. Drew was a recipient of the Bucks County Muse Award in 2016 for contributions to the Bucks County PA literary community. His biography appears in *Mississippi Poets: A Literary Guide*, U of Mississippi Press, edited by Catherine Savage Brosman. In 2019 Drew collaborated with singer/songwriter Rick Kunz on a CD of original poetry and songs entitled *A Triumph of Loneliness*, KBW Music.

One Winter Midnight on the Delta

I dread the color of the answer Yes.
—Bill Knott

Shadows. Firelit shadows on a delta winter night;
      under his blanket, shadows the boy considers.

    The boy is on the sofa, an old and moldy,
dog hair-permeated wreck of a sofa someone set

      out on their lawn with a hand-printed sign:
Take It—Free. Shadows, and for the boy the only

Freedom—sleep. And sleep is anywhere anytime away
      from what he hears: from their bedroom

    Mama's no no no and Daddy's yes yes yes
streaming like rancid air bled out of black balloons,

      headboard banging and behind the plyboard wall
bees threatening retaliation. Through the gates

of half-closed eyelids Daddy slides like oil,
      like shadow over the rugless floor, a naked shadow,

    what's between its legs thick, veined and violent.
Beside the boy Daddy stops, hovers, spreads

      like shadow, like black moonlight at midnight
blanketing his blanket, him. No, the boy implores,

      Oh no no no. Yes, Daddy's shadow whispers, Oh yes.

Elegy: Rolling Fork

Oh, Rolling Fork, my Rolling Fork,

I'm still here, one of the survivors said,
and so was my Aunt Lil, still there in Rolling Fork
back then, she and her dozen kids; back then,
the town itself was just a cluster of typical
Mississippi small, white clapboard homes
and, though it's all a bit foggy after all these years,
a grocery, a café or two, a gas station and a bank.

Oh, Rolling Fork, my Rolling Fork,

more than once, I remember, Mama
drove us from Clarksdale to Aunt Lil's for a visit,
my brother and sister and me; I don't
remember much of anything about those visits,
what we said and did, but on the *Evening News*
they say that a tornado has flattened Rolling Fork,
that in fact Rolling Fork is no more.

Oh, Rolling Fork, my Rolling Fork,

more than my long-ago departed Aunt Lil,
I find myself grieving the survivor, that he's still
here when in fact his *here* no longer is;
that all I see is piles of rubble, tossed trucks,
trees stripped of branches, water tower
down, and a man with a suitcase just
stumbling along; that even the ghosts are gone.

Oh, Rolling Fork, my Rolling Fork . . .

Don't Tell Me the Universe Doesn't Have a Sense of Humor

One reason you can't go home again is that you never leave it.
—Jack Crocker

Want, want, want—I hear it everywhere . . .

And me? I want to be back in the white duplex
with its porch unscreened and tree-shadowed
across the street from Ella Darling School
in Greenville, Mississippi in the summer
of my tenth year; I want to be there again,
even when I bicycled into the rear end of a car
near the Paramount Theater and rolled
over the top of the car, over the hood and down,
deposited on the pavement in front of the car.

Want, want, want—I hear it everywhere . . .

And me? I want to be back in the heat and humidity
of that Mississippi summer, even though that
was when one morning Bonita Stanton, the first
girl I ever thought I was in love with, shot me
in the ass with her brother's BB gun;
I want to again be skipping across the lawn
of Ella Darling School and humming a country tune,
even after a bigger boy's line drive smacked me
in the head and sent me somewhere over the moon.

Want, want, want—I hear it everywhere . . .

And me? Mostly, I want to again take out after
the old black man who had my sister
by the arm and was dragging her and her screams
down the street and away from the white duplex,
my grandmother yelling and me shouting at him
to let, let, let my sister go; mostly, that is,
for that one unmitigated Mississippi moment
I want to be the hero my grandmother said I was;
even more, I want to be the hero I never was.

The Devil Took a Midnight Train

The sun rose on the mountain
redder than a drunken eye
as the devil told his demons
he was off to Georgia, goodbye.

It's true, ya'll, the devil took
a midnight train and when it crossed
the Georgia line took out his fiddle
and played so hard the strings

begun to snap like twine,
and when that Hellbound train
pulled into the depot
the devil rosined up his bow,

said he was gonna rock the joint
all night and into day,
and work his fiddle hotter
than a griddle. O yippie ki yea!

Yessir, the devil was the best
and if that long-haired,
Hellbound Carolina boy
dared to take the devil's dare,

to risk his legendary name,
to pull his musty fiddle
from its musty case
and show up, hey diddle, diddle,

and take him on again, why then,
the devil would show him
no downhome mama's boy would
ever outplay the Cloven One.

And so it was the devil begun
to ready his golden bow
and fire up his fiddle there
on the platform of that depot.

For days the devil cooled his feet
waiting for Charlie D to show,
but what he didn't know
was Charlie'd hopped a freight

headed due north to Paradise
and with a choir of harps backin'
down his fiery fiddle
wouldn't ever be heard from again.

What could the Foul One do?
Charlie'd done flew the coop,
and all the devil got was
a bad bad case of hellish croup.

DENISE DUHAMEL's most recent books of poetry are *Second Story* (Pittsburgh, 2021) and *Scald* (2017). *Blowout* (2013) was a finalist for the National Book Critics Circle Award. A proponent of collaboration, she and Maureen Seaton have co-authored five collections, the most recent of which is *CAPRICE (Collaborations: Collected, Uncollected, and New)* (Sibling Rivalry Press, 2015). Her nonfiction publications include *The Unrhymables: Collaborations in Prose* (with Julie Marie Wade, Noctuary Press, 2019). She also served as a guest editor for *The Best American Poetry 2013*. A recipient of fellowships from the Guggenheim Foundation and the National Endowment for the Arts, Duhamel is a distinguished university professor in the MFA program at Florida International University.

Fortunately, Unfortunately, Florida

Fortunately, I live by the sea.
Unfortunately, the sea is dying.
Fortunately, for me, the blob of seaweed is on the west coast.
Unfortunately, the east coast of Florida where I live has sharks.
Fortunately, the sharks prefer to eat other fish.
Unfortunately, overfishing has wiped out a lot of shark meals.
Fortunately, lifeguards keep watch from 10-6.
Unfortunately, those lifeguards are often distracted, on their phones.
Fortunately, phones provide charts about jellyfish blooms.
Unfortunately, a jellyfish can float away from the others.
Fortunately, pink moon jellies are easy for humans to spot.
Unfortunately, clear comb jellyfish are sometimes undetectable.
Fortunately, most jellyfish stings cause pain and swelling, but that's
      about it.
Unfortunately, the stings of certain box jellies (or sea wasps) are fatal.
Fortunately, the pain of most stings can be relieved with vinegar.
Unfortunately, some people think human urine will help.
Fortunately, this myth makes for some good jokes.
Unfortunately, some of those jokes will be banned if our Governor has
      anything to say about it.
Fortunately, some banned books gain a wider readership.
Unfortunately, the Governor wants to ban AP Black history courses.
Fortunately, students are making impromptu study groups, teaching
      themselves.
Unfortunately, impromptu study groups are not available to everyone.
Fortunately, abortion is still available in some states.
Unfortunately, abortion is restricted to six weeks in Florida.
Fortunately, I kept my "Keep Abortion Safe and Legal" bumper sticker
      from the 70s.
Unfortunately, that bumper sticker is relevant again.
Fortunately, I still feel relevant when I write about these things.
Unfortunately, I sometimes feel scared to write what I feel.
Fortunately, I'm still feeling something.
Unfortunately, I feel rage and fear because of the latest mass shooting.
Fortunately—well, there aren't many fortunate things to say about guns.

Unfortunately, I'm feeling outnumbered by bigots.

Fortunately, my rational brain knows there are more of my kind than theirs.

Unfortunately, more drag queens and LGBTQ+ folk are under attack.

Fortunately, they have senses of humor—*Rhonda DeSatan, keep drag queens safe from children!*

Unfortunately, Ron isn't gracious when it comes to laughing at himself.

Fortunately, Ron's rigid thinking would make him lose at improv.

Unfortunately, over 2000 sea creatures are threatened according to the Endangered Species Act.

Fortunately, it's sunny today with wild waves—and I am a creature who loves the sea.

Poem in Which I Give Up and Embrace Keats

I moved to Florida in 1999, moved into an apartment
on the beach, confident Al Gore would be elected. I mean,
who would vote for a dolt like George? Sure,
Gore could have done more when he wobbled
about protecting the Everglades, causing some to jump
ship and throw in with Ralph Nader. I know Ralph
would have been a better president than either
Al or George, but we all know what happens
to third party candidates. In 2000 there was still
a little time to turn this ship around, the ship
the Nader voters jumped from. On election night
I went to dinner thinking Al had won, but by dessert
the restaurant TV was saying George demanded
a recount. Wall Street types—organized by Roger
Stone—marched in Miami, and Florida became
the butt of "hanging chad" jokes. The Supreme
Court overruled the Florida Supreme Court
to stop a recount of the votes in four
Florida counties. *Howdy, George.* Now it's 2022
and the ocean inches closer while Joe Manchin
looks the other way. Speaking of ships, Joe
was on his yacht when constituents rowed
towards him in protest, begging him to get on board
with Biden's Build Back Better. Joe's betting
his money on coal, hoping Elon Musk
will take him on his spaceship to Mars.
Today I am tired of fighting, tired
of wringing my hands. I don't have to tell you
what happened next—the World Trade Center,
unjustified wars, the crash of 2008, more oil spills,
then Trump. Now there's inflation,
the overturning of Roe v. Wade, the insurrection
hearings. Everyone's seemed to have forgotten
about the environment, that it's 104 degrees
today in London with train tracks buckling,

cars overheating. Airstrips softened by extreme heat
have grounded the Royal Air Force. Wildfires
spread through the Mediterranean.
Portugal's temperature is 116. And here, in the U.S.,
in Hawaii, 20-foot-high waves
crashed onto the shore and over highways.
Colorado, Texas, Oklahoma and Arkansas
all breaking records for high temperatures
under something called a heat dome. I'm thinking
of Mad Max's Thunderdome or the earth
as a dead pheasant under a silver cloche.
I'll probably rally tomorrow and be ready
to fight again, but for today my rant ends here.
You'll find me running into the sea,
me and my culpability, my negative capability.

Display

My mother's scoliosis has her leaning
the same way as the palm trees behind her.
She's still standing on her own
wearing the pink lipstick she gave to me
and I wear now. A yellow shirt is hard
to pull off if you are pale
and my mom is pale in this photo,
but she looks beautiful, her silver bangs
in the breeze, a palm like a feather in her hair.
And there I am, too, tiny, in the double lenses
of her sunglasses—my torso, my white shirt,
my arms lifting my camera phone. Beyond
her, the lifeguard hut flaps a green flag
which tells us the waves are mild today
but for years my mother has been too wobbly
to navigate sand. Beyond her shoulder
is her walker which I rented at Locatel
Health and Wellness so she wouldn't have to
lug her own. An employee from Southwest
wheeled her to baggage claim
where I met her. My mother was embarrassed
and gave the woman who pushed her a big tip.
Then I wheeled her to the parking garage,
my mother's suitcase across her lap.
The yellow shirt is my shirt now, but it looks awful
on me. I'll donate it to Goodwill as soon as I can
part with it. My mother once made crazy quilts
and ate kiddie ice cream cups with a wooden spoon.
That is when she could still sit up. That is when
her hands still worked. I transfer this photo
to a thumb drive and take it to CVS.
The man who prints it out says
What a striking woman. And it strikes me
then—all the mourners will say something
about this photo we display atop the closed casket.

My Mother's Cover-Up

I bought one for her at Walgreens—teal blue with sparkles. She was so hunched over and short by then, it flowed almost to her ankles. I kept it here in Florida so that when she visited it was one less thing she needed to pack. It was in a drawer along with her one-piece, skirted bathing suit which had adjustable shoulder straps to accommodate her lopsidedness, her scoliosis. Now that she's gone, I wear the cover-up and mourn each loose sequin, trying to catch them as they fall. Walgreens doesn't sell this kind of kaftan anymore—if it did, I would buy more as a way to keep my mother with me. I walk the seasonal aisle as though it's a metaphor for life itself. Plastic pails and shovels to make dreamy castles, water shoes to protect our feet from rocks, and neon noodles to help keep us afloat.

After the Tropical Storm

I walk into the Atlantic, the silt so soft
I feel like I'm trudging through mud.
I begin to swim towards the horizon. It is then
I see the baby loggerheads, newly hatched,
the size of quarters, paddling beside me.
When they swerve, I swerve. When they bob
on the surface, so do I. My mother
has just died. I follow the turtles
for two miles at which point I become
one of them, or they one of me, our shells hardening.
We eat kelp and fish eggs, keep each other company.
We grow and have babies of our own.
Theirs are inside eggs. Mine are inside little poems.

KENDALL DUNKELBERG directs the low-residency MFA in Creative Writing and the Eudora Welty Writers' Symposium at Mississippi University for Women. Born and raised in Iowa, he has lived in Belgium, Texas, and Illinois before moving to Mississippi nearly thirty years ago to teach. He was an early participant in slam poetry at the Green Mill Lounge in Chicago, then earned his PhD in Comparative Literature from the University of Texas at Austin. He is editor of *Poetry South* and has published three collections of poetry, *Barrier Island Suite*, *Time Capsules*, and *Landscapes and Architectures*, as well as a translation of Flemish poems by Paul Snoek, *Hercules, Richelieu, and Nostradamus*, and the textbook, *A Writer's Craft: Multi-genre Creative Writing*. Dunkelberg has been the featured poet at *Delta Poetry Review* and *Valley Voices*, and his work has recently appeared in *Birmingham Poetry Review*, *Juke Joint*, *River Mouth Review*, and *Peauxdunque Review*. His fourth collection of poems, *Tree Fall with Birdsong* will be published in May 2025 by Fernwood Press.

Acknowledgments

"*Beso con Lengua*"
     First appeared in *Poetry South*
"Continental Divide"
     First appeared in *Valley Voices*
"Patterns"
     First appeared in *The Cape Rock*
"Cathedral"
     First appeared in *Delta Poetry Review*
"Birdsong"
     First appeared in *Tar River Poetry*

Beso con Lengua

Back when I lived in Chicago and still ate meat,
my roommates and I loved to go to *taquerias*,
where you could get real barrio food, not
the Americanized fare that passes for Mexican
in Mississippi. Yet my roommates never
dared to try my favorite, *tacos con lengua*,
a cross-cultural glossolalia wrapped in tortilla.

Tongue wasn't so foreign to me. My mother grew up
eating it on the farm and passed it on to us, buying
gigantic beef tongues, studding them with cloves
and boiling them in her biggest stock pot. We loved
to eat it hot with horseradish or cold in a sandwich,
the sensation of the cow's big, tender taste buds
on our own was our favorite part, a culinary French kiss
long before we became aware of the opposite sex.

Still, now that I've moved to the South, I'm glad
I've become a vegetarian. I don't have to draw
the line at chitlins: somehow, intestine on intestine
doesn't have quite the allure of tongue touching tongue.
And I really have no desire to suck the flesh from
between the toes of a pig, pickled or otherwise.

Yet I have to admire the honesty of using
every part of the animal you eat, in the way
that as a boy I admired the idea of the Get Smart
Sandwich at the drive-in in Belle Plaine, Iowa,
but never could quite stomach the reality
of scrambled brains on a sesame bun.

Continental Divide

Rte. 52 near Hibbing, Minnesota

If a drop of rain would fall,
where would it travel?
To the west of this spot
it would flow to icy Hudson Bay;
half an inch further south takes
it to the balmy Gulf; a hair
to the east, and it would flow
down into Lake Superior.

We are not like that raindrop.
We travel over the divide here
in Minnesota without a thought.
It is barely a rise with only
a marker to tell we've crossed
from one watershed to another
our fluidity so much greater and
less consequential than water.

For of course the sign is wrong.
If one drop of water were to fall,
it would soak into the ground,
traveling down to join the aquifer or up
the roots and stem of a prairie flower.
It would take a million drops, a
downpour to flow in all directions,
wearing the continent away here
and extending it at the sea.

Patterns

This stone holds the pattern
of fossilized fern, its amber
leaflets still recognizable after
eons, though the rock has been
crushed and cemented in the path
where now an orange and green
nearly black, box turtle ambles
across, as yesterday an antlered
young buck crossed the river, a black
lab hard on its heels as he swam
to the other bank then ran
along it, headed back, but turned tail
afraid of the dog who wagged
much like the ponytail of the blond
jogger that flips in front of me and
is followed by an old man
whose indigo tattoo waves
on his arm, a sign of his war,
the way the fern must have
waved in its wind or the buck
tossed his antlers before rising
out of the water, safe on his side
of the river for now. What
is mortality in the face
of this life, stretching for ages
along a path, both future and past
and what are our fantasies
of immortality, when daily
the patterns are reenacted.

Cathedral

After the night of heavy storms
along the swollen creek banks
cypress knees wave peace signs
at the universe. The sun dawns
calm and yellow, as water runs off
in rivulets, surveying the land.

But for a few downed limbs
it would be hard not to imagine
that last night's winds and sheets
of rain were but a dream, a childish
nightmare, hard not to believe in
the promise of the tooth fairy, that
out of pain comes something good.

Listen to the birds in the trees:
you cannot see them, but believe
their song. Look at the early sun
falling through the cathedral arches
of trunks and branches. Feel
a gentle breeze caress your cheek.

Birdsong

The magpie gathers all
that sparkles. He is a thief
or a garbage man.
He speaks to everything
in its own tongue.

◊◊◊

Why, when the heron
flies, does he let his feet
dangle below his wide,
graceful wings? Is it to
keep his balance, to steer
like a ship, or could it be
the heron loves to feel
the air rush deliciously
between his toes.

◊◊◊

I could try to write of the flickers
but I never saw more than one
of their the maple-colored tails
fanned out in flight. You saw two
of them, a couple, lit on the trunk
of a tree, their heads bobbing
in unison, both searching for food.

◊◊◊

This spring I see two brown thrashers
flying together as one ball of feathers
a creature with four wings and two
tails in constant motion for a moment
until they break apart, and I discern

the female as one distinct bird,
the male close behind, pestering.
Now I see them one at a time
flitting in and out of the red camellia,
one on guard as the other broods.

JO ANGELA EDWINS has published poems in over 100 journals and anthologies, recently or forthcoming in *The Hollins Critic, Capsule Stories, Shō Poetry Journal,* and *Pirene's Fountain.* Her chapbook, *Play,* was published in 2016 by Finishing Line Press, and her full-length collection, *A Dangerous Heaven,* was published in 2023 by Gnashing Teeth Publishing. She has received awards from Winning Writers, Poetry Super Highway, The Jasper Project, and the South Carolina Academy of Authors and is a Pushcart Prize, Forward Prize, and Bettering American Poetry nominee. A native of North Augusta, SC, Edwins lives in Florence, SC, where she teaches at Francis Marion University and serves as the first poet laureate of the Pee Dee region of the state.

House of Hubcaps

Mel's Tires, Florence, SC

The building leans a bit. No doubt the weight
of so much chrome unsettles foundations,
tilts old timbers. Even the chain link guarding
the yard wears them like medals, like
a giant superhero's garish bling. You wonder
most at the ones hanging high,
lining the chimney to the gable's apex,
the effort it took to hook there
hubcap after hubcap, overlapping
like terracotta shingles, these silver circles
sparkling in late afternoon sun.
What's left to see of the house's siding
has gone gray now, or black, or rust.
But who looks at that? The rest is the miracle,
sculptural, an industrial witch's cottage.
So many radials stripped of their dressing,
armor abandoned to rain and wind
that hardly dim the spark. Imagine too
the hours of deals to acquire them. Or was it labor
of love, walking highways, mad intersections,
hotbeds of collision, where what is lost
none dare reclaim? Picture Mel,
if you know him, if he exists, wading, fishing
a weedy ditch for lost relics of fender-benders
or pothole casualties, old journeys resurrected
in dingy alloys he will polish to the sheen
of a thousand mirrors reflecting each Southern summer
from across the street a phone booth, that magically
still holds a wired phone, its bright black receiver
hooked by silver circles to the whole spinning world.

At a Hotel Rooftop Bar in My Hometown

North Augusta, SC

My friends and I count church spires
across the river in the city where I was born.
We smell the heady smoke of hickory fires
from the restaurant below. The river bank, shorn
of the oak and hackberry I knew as a child,
now sports a baseball stadium, a promenade,
and here and there a sapling growing wild
by landscaper's accident or the strange grace of God,
and everywhere are people walking dogs,
feeding meters, waiting in line for food,
staring at phones, too high to see the frogs
and turtles below them, their natural attitude
focused as always on living, producing young.
(I can't see them either, although I hope they're there.)
Above our heads electric lights, artfully strung,
begin to glow. A slight chill invades the air.
We leave the balcony, move back to the warmer bar,
where the stools face the hotel wall, veneered with stone.
A burnt-wood sign declares simply, "Here you are."
The river flows behind us, not quite as it's always done.

A Car Has Collided with a Cow on West Cummings Road in Timmonsville

Facebook post by a television reporter in Florence, SC
February 1, 2023

I hope you feel sorry for the cow
before you feel any urge to laugh.
I hope you then feel a little guilty for thinking
of the people in the car second.
But the only flesh-and-blood mentioned in the sentence
is that of the cow, noble in her humility,
in her mundanity (and now I'm distracted
from grief for the cow's pain, wondering
if "mundanity" is a word). How often in my life
I've written a word and wondered if it was real.
How often in my life I've mourned the death of those
whose kind have died a thousand times
and I never thought twice about them.
Today for lunch I ate a hamburger.
Today, after waiting for seven minutes
for a passing train, I judged the distance between
a pulsing ambulance and my fresh green light
and gunned the engine. The ambulance was not that close,
but I should have waited anyway. I should
have given the driver space to trust
a clear path between human need
and the distant promise of help.
I should have honored the fact
that even those collisions that shatter
only the peace of the mind's eye
should probably never happen
since any violence—real or imagined,
accidental or deliberate—takes
our precious breath away. I feel
as if there should be more to say,
but I'm not sure what. Life thrives
on this confusion, things barreling down upon us

like an ambulance, closer than we think.
Like a cow, faster than we think.
We must keep our eyes open
for safety's sake, sure, but also
we have so little time
and so much of this mad earth yet to see.

Atomic Bomb Accident at Mars Bluff, SC, March 11, 1958

Anymore the world ticks faster
than father's wristwatch, the one brought back
from a land turned dirt and crumbled concrete,
ashen faces, air tasting of stone.

Here we are young. Here we play
fairy games in an old-growth wood,
plucking dewberries with grimy fingers,
swallowing the grit with the juice.

It landed on the playhouse,

that place where we acted at being grown,
stirring weeds and twigs in chipped crockery.
Sometimes we chafed like our parents
at each other, at imaginary children.

But no more. So much splintered wood
and a crater like a pock on the moon,
smooth and new-skinned. Our wounds would heal
in time, the thing our father's watch

kept once, before this. Before he snapped it
from his wrist like a serpent, revealing a circle
seared red from the heat, as if God himself
reached down from the white sky and gripped him tighter

than an angry parent, and never let go.

Clearing Out the House

East Tennessee, 1935

My mother never told me
what they chose to save
and what they left behind.
Hand-hewn furniture,
frayed linens, cracked cups.
Did they take it all,
or only what would fit
in the sputtering truck?
I am imagining the truck,
as I doubt my grandfather owned one.
I am imagining everything here.

She would have been nine.
She would not have understood
how men could build a dam
to build a lake. She had always been taught
that God shaped the planet
the way her father shaped walking canes
with chisel and knife, his hands
looming wide and powerful.

How would they know
that where they went
would remain dry?
Would they count the days
until another man in suit and tie
ordered them to abandon the land?
How her mother must have cried,
tucking children, chickens, blankets
in whatever spaces would hold them,
hiding a handful of photographs
in the bosom of her dress.

Soon enough the rooms in which
she brought her children into the world
would be yards beneath the water.
In time the dark lake's weight and wetness
would make roof and wall collapse.
No one would know just when.
No one would care. By then,
they would be digging the soil
of a different mountain
across the state line. The mother,
sick in a cruel winter, would die
and be carried back to lie in a cemetery
on the dry side of the ridge,
and the floors they swept
and the doors they opened and closed
would no longer be the hardest of things
to which they had had to say goodbye.

BETH ANN FENNELLY, a 2020 Academy of American Poets Laureate Fellow, was the poet laureate of Mississippi from 2016-2021 and teaches in the MFA Program at the University of Mississippi. She's won numerous grants and awards, including those from the United States Artists and the National Endowment for the Arts, in addition to a Pushcart Prize and a Fulbright grant to Brazil. She has published three books of poetry and three of prose, most recently, *Heating & Cooling: 52 Micro-Memoirs*. Fennelly lives with her husband, the novelist Tom Franklin (with whom she co-wrote *The Tilted World*), and their three children in Oxford, MS. Website: https://www.bethannfennelly.com/.

Acknowledgments

"First Warm Day in a College Town"
      First published in *The Oxford American*, reprinted in
      Unmentionables (W. W. Norton)
"I Need to Be More French. Or Japanese."
      First published in *Ploughshares*, reprinted in *Tender Hooks*
      (W. W. Norton)
"The Last Hummingbird"
      First published in *POETRY*, reprinted in *The Ecopoetry*
      Anthology: Volume II
"Because People Ask What My Daughter Will Think of My Poems When She's Sixteen"
      First published in *The Southeast Review*, reprinted in
      Unmentionables (W. W. Norton)
"Why I Can't Cook for Your Self-Centered Architect Cousin"
      First published in *The New Great American Writers*
      Cookbook, reprinted in *The Bitter Southerner* and *Open House*
      (W. W. Norton)

First Warm Day in a College Town

Today is the day the first bare-chested
  runners appear, coursing down College Hill
    as I drive to campus to teach, hard

not to stare because it's only February 15,
  and though I now live in the South, I spent
    my girlhood in frigid Illinois hunting Easter eggs

in snow, or trick-or-treating in the snow, an umbrella
  protecting my cardboard wings, so now it's hard
    not to see these taut colts as my reward, these yearlings

testing the pasture, hard as they come toward my Nissan
  not to turn my head as they pound past, hard
    not to angle the mirror to watch them cruise

down my shoulder, too hard, really, when I await them
  like crocuses, search for their shadows as others do
    the groundhog's, and suddenly here they are, the boys

without shirts, how fleet of foot,
  how cute their buns,
    I have made it again, it is spring.

Hard to recall just now that these are the torsos
  of my students, or my past or future students, who every year
    grow one year younger, get one year fewer

of my funny jokes and hip references
  to *Fletch* and Nirvana, which means some year if they catch me
    admiring, they won't grin grins that make me, busted,

grin back—hard to know a spring will come
  when I'll have to train my eyes
    on the dash, the fuel gauge nearing empty,

hard to think of that spring, that
      distant spring, that very very very (please God)
        distant spring.

I Need to Be More French. Or Japanese.

Then I wouldn't prefer the California wine,
its big sugar, big fruit rolling down my tongue,
a cornucopia spilled across a tacky tablecloth.
I'd prefer the French, its smoke and rot.
Said Cézanne: *Le mond—c'est terrible!*
Which means, *The world—it bites the big weenie.*
People sound smarter in French.
The Japanese prefer the crescent moon to the full,
prefer the rose before it blooms.
Oh, I have been to the temples of Kyoto,
I have stood on the Pont Neuf, and my eyes,
they drank it in, but my taste buds
shuffled along in the beer line at Wrigley Field.
It was the day they gave out foam fingers.
I hereby pledge to wear more gray, less yellow
of the beaks of baby mockingbirds,
that huge yellow yawping open on wobbly necks,
trusting something yummy will be dropped inside,
soon. I hereby pledge to be reserved.
When the French designer learned
I didn't like her mockups for my book cover,
she sniffed, *They're not for everyone. They're
subtle. What area code is 662 anyway?* I said,
*Mississippi, sweetheart. Bet you couldn't find it
with a map.* Okay: I didn't really. But so what
if I'm subtle as May in Mississippi, my nose
in the wine-bowl of this magnolia bloom, so what
if I'm mellow as the punch-drunk bee.
If I were Japanese I'd write about magnolias
in March, how tonal, each bud long as a pencil,
sheathed in celadon suede, jutting from a cluster
of glossy leaves. I'd end the poem before anything
bloomed, end with rain swelling the buds
and the sheaths bursting, then falling to the grass
like a fairy's castoff slippers, like candy wrappers,

like spent firecrackers. Yes, my poem
would end there, spent firecrackers.
If I were French, I'd capture post-peak, in July,
the petals floppy, creased brown with age,
the stamens naked, stripped of yellow filaments.
The bees lazy now, bungling the ballet, thinking
for the first time about October. If I were French,
I'd prefer this, end with red-tipped filaments
scattered on the scorched brown grass,
and my poem would incite the sophisticated,
the French and Japanese readers—
because the filaments look like matchsticks,
and it's matchsticks, we all know, that start the fire.

The Last Hummingbird of Summer

reveals itself in retrospect. Unlike the first,
whose March arrival bade you gasp, hands clasped,
like a child actor instructed to show joy, when the last
departs for points south, there's no telling,
and no tell. Well, so what? You know their cycle.
In August, they swarm the feeder, all swagger,
greedy tussle for sugar water. Suddenly,
September. Chill tickles your ankles. You reach
for long sleeves and you fret. They've left? Not yet.
Ear cocked for the symphony's shrinking strings.
Then comes a day without a ruby flash. Next day,
they're back. Next day, there's one. Then none.
Or maybe one? From porches, pumpkins grin.
Your last had left, and left you uninformed.

Kinda? Sorta? Can I say it?—like menstrual blood,
again, between your legs. Your last, perhaps,
or next-to-last, your no-longer-very-monthly
monthly. So unlike your first crimson, at twelve,
its "Yes-You-*Are*-There-God" annunciation.
Well, so what? You know the cycle. Your body's
eggy miracle, unneeded now for years.
And you hate waste. Why fill and dump
and fill again the undrunk sugar water?
Enough. Let's progress to whatever season's next.
But still, a farewell ritual wouldn't be amiss.
The last hummingbird of summer, zinging
from the feeder—to others, a smooth departure—
to you, alone, unmistakably, dipping its wing.

Because People Ask What My Daughter Will Think of My Poems When She's Sixteen

Daughter, the light of
the future is apricot,
and in it you are not
the thigh-child pointing
her earnest index finger
to the yellow balloon clearing
the willows and drifting
higher, you're the balloon. I'm
the grasping hand. Or I'm
the *oo* in *balloon*. I'll meet you
there. I'm the brown
strings, formerly violets, you
didn't water. I'm the hole
in the photo, you're the un-
safety scissors. I'm the lint
in the corners of my purse
after you steal the coins,
brown-bag lunch you pitch
after leaving my house, buttons
you undo after I've okayed
your blouse. Poems
you burn in the sink. Poems
that had to go and use
your name, never mind
that soon you'll be sixteen, hate
your name. I'm the resemblance
you deny, fat ass
you hope your boyfriends
never see. I'll meet you
there, that is my promise
and my threat, with this
yellow balloon as my
witness, even if I'm
dead, I'll meet you there.

Why I Can't Cook for Your Self-Centered Architect Cousin

Because to me, a dinner table's like a bed—
without love, it's all appetite and stains. Let's buy
take-out for your cousin, or order pizza—his toppings—

but I can't lift a spatula to serve him what I am.
Instead, invite our favorite misfits over: I'll feed
shaggy Otis who, after filet mignon, raised his plate

and sipped merlot sauce with such pleasure
my ego pardoned his manners. Or I'll call Mimi,
the chubby librarian, who paused over tiramisu—

"I haven't felt so satisfied since . . ." then cried
into its curls of chocolate. Or Randolph might stop by,
who once, celebrating his breakup with the vegan,

so packed the purse seine of his wiry body with shrimp
he unbuttoned his jeans and spent the evening
couched, "waiting for the swelling to go down."

Or maybe I'll just cook for us. I'll crush pine nuts
unhinged from the cones' prickly shingles.
I'll whittle the parmesan, and if I grate a knuckle

it's just more of me in my cooking. I'll disrobe
garlic cloves of rosy sheaths, thresh the basil
till moist, and liberate the oil. Then I'll dance

that green joy through the fettuccine, a tumbling,
leggy dish we'll imitate, after dessert.
If my embrace detects the five pounds you win

each year, you will merely seem a generous
portion. And if you bring my hand to your lips
and smell the garlic that lingers, that scents

the sweat you lick from the hollows of my clavicles,
you're tasting the reason that I can't cook
for your cousin—my saucy, my strongly seasoned love.

LYMAN GRANT was born in Birmingham, Alabama, graduated high school in Temple, Texas, and has degrees from both the University of Texas and Texas A&M University. For over forty years he taught at Austin Community College, where he also served as Dean of the Arts and Humanities Division. In retirement, he lives in the Shenandoah Valley in Virginia. His poems and essays have appeared in numerous journals and anthologies, including *Texas Observer*, *Dallas Morning News*, *Texas Books in Review*, *Langdon Review*, *Concho River Review*, *descant*, *Windhover*, *Compstock Review*, *Cider Press Review*, *Literary Austin*, *Written in Arlington*, *Soul X Southwest*, *Chaos Dive Reunion*, *Unknotting the Line*, *Bearing the Mask*, *Whitman 200*, and *The Great American Wise Ass Anthology*. He has published several volumes of poems, most recently *Symptom and Desire: New and Selected Poems* and *ostraca*, a volume of golden shovel poems. In 2024, Grant will publish his tenth volume, *November Constellation*. He can be found on the web at 4doorlounge.com.

Acknowledgments

"Pedestal"
> Published previously in *ROPES* (University of Galway) and in *Symptom and Desire: New and Selected Poems*

Old Man's Breakfast at Cracker Barrel

I.
For the third time, no, the fourth,
two golf tees remain in the wooden
triangle. He remembers a time
forty years ago when he would
quickly decimate every tee
but the final one left standing
firm in its worn hole as if he were
holding an automatic in his back-forty
shooting range, the line of cans
and bottles jumping and exploding.
Now he plods his way, the hair
on his neck erect, as if trekking
the edge of a wood waiting to flush
a covey of quail across the field.
Slowly the tees collect on the pine
table, stained yellow Southern oak,
but always a few avoid his aim.

II.
He knows his cardiologist
will have sharp words for him.
The eggs sunny side up swimming
in fat, the hash brown casserole
smothered in cheddar, sprinkled
with bacon crumbles. He did
forego the pork gravy and requested
Impossible sausage instead of his
favorite Virginia ham. Surely, a man
can't be expected to give up all
of his pleasures and memories:
his mother's large and hardy
breakfasts made to keep her boys
filled and fueled for their high
school sports and outdoor labor.
He butters up that fluffy biscuit
and slathers jam, sweet and thick.

III.

Today's waitress—yes, he still uses
that word with no apparent discomfort—
trim, efficient, hair proudly gray—
refills his decaf one last time,
and the old man relaxes in his hard chair,
breathes in a misplaced and forgotten
comfort—fading magazine pages
from the Depression, *Child's Life*
covers celebrating Valentine's
and Thanksgiving, ads for Weston
SuperX 22 shells and farm plows,
rusted metal signs for Triple AAA
Root Beer and Dr. Lyna's Hair Grower,
etched scenes of hounds on the hunt,
and a large black and white framed
photograph of a young couple
posed in nascent dignity, sitting
closely on a bench in the photographer's
studio. The photo perhaps served
to announce their final transition into
adult life. *We are married*, they announce,
*we are adults, we tempt this world
to view of us as such*. He in his dark
suit, she in her white dress.
He with his tie pinned high, she
with her bouquet. He with his right hand
on his left leg leaning toward her,
she serene, both hands clasped in
a satisfied lap. The old man studies
the photograph, lifts himself from
his chair and hunts into the eyes
of this young man, this young woman.
Her eyes say everything will be all right.
His eyes say, I hope so.

IV.

In the lobby, before he pays the price
of his indulgence, the old man wanders
the aisles of country kitsch, mugs

for the World's Greatest Grandad,
sequined t-shirts, pre-internet children's
toys, Goo-Goo candy bars, and ValloMilk
Cups. Outside, he lingers. The sun
has risen high in the eastern sky. Light
has warmed the restaurant porch.
Today, why not, he sits in one
of the rocking chairs lined up facing
the parking lot, and above the highway
that Eisenhower built and some Democrat
raised taxes to repair. He nods, lifts
a scarred hand, and smiles at old couples
and businessmen hurrying past
for their early lunch. "Good day,"
he says, and really means it. This afternoon,
watching his favorite Westerns,
he'll unwrap that MoonPie he just bought,
content that some things no matter
the year remain the same.

Bottle Tree

When the moon is full
and its stark eye sparkles
the dark cobalt glass,
exuberant spirits rise
from their secret dens

in fascinated thrall
to enter the open mouths
of dazzle's snare.
Listen closely. In morning's
emergence, they buzz

their ecstatic repentance,
intoning health, wealth,
and unceasing pleasures,
as sunlight flares their nasty
wings to silence and ash.

Blossoms the Color of Joy

When I die, if asked, I'd like
to return as a dogwood tree.
I'd request to be placed in front
of a small clapboard house, paint
beginning to fleck, say, about fifty
feet back from a gravel country road.
Maybe off to one side is a rusted
truck up on blocks. Plant me

so that the family can see me
from the living room windows
and remember such a thing as hope
when bills are high and the cupboard
is low. If it is not asking too much,
I'd like a couple of tall oaks
or sweet gums nearby to shade me,
please? It can get tough out there,

but I will do my best, regardless.
Mostly, I think about the young boy
in the house and how he might
watch me through all the seasons
year after year: Spring's white
blossoms like velvet butterflies,
a cool dappled shade in summer,
crimson and yellow leaves in fall.

In winter I will stand bare, arms
extended like a dancer's stretching
grace into God's lonely, abandoned
spaces. I hope he would notice
finally that every season gifts its own
special joy, but that spring, glorious
spring, can be counted on to return
no matter what winter has brought.

Pedestal

Robert E. Lee at the University of Texas
And I am spent with old wars and new sorrow.
—Donald Davidson, *Lee in the Mountains*, 1865-1870

Most don't even notice me beneath these oaks.
They trudge past, weighted down by deadlines and backpacks,
hunched like soldiers shaped by burdens they bear for . . . what?
For honor? Glory? A parent's or professor's
praise? For wealth, greed? All that was mine, once, long ago.
But now I wait, immobile, paralyzed, like Grant
had me pinned in Petersburg. From this pedestal
tucked in shade between old Rainey and Calhoun Halls
I've seen it all, the calls to take me down, the pleas
to cut the present from its past, the tears, the shouts,
a face uplifted, stiffly proud, defiant, bold,
urging me, as at Appomattox, to fight on.
It's not my fight. I never wanted civil strife.

I did my duty. They forget the years I rode
in Texas, living on boiled meat and molasses,
battered by sun and wind and frontier loneliness,
a desert of dullness. Fort Mason, Camp Cooper,
Fort Chadbourne, Ringgold Barracks, Fort Brown, Fort Duncan,
San Antonio, Castroville, miles upon miles
on horseback, serving these United States, chasing
ghosts, Comanches and bandits. Honor as empty
as creek beds. No one celebrates men who do dull
work dutifully. I did not rate pedestals
back then. My sad letters home: *No grass for horses,*
no shadows for men. What a blessed thing the children
are not here. They would be ruined. As I was ruined.

One morning here, sun rose upon the old message
in a new phrase, *Black Lives Matter* quickly painted
on my granite stand, sprayed in flash attack like John
Brown at Harper's Ferry, another step toward

irrevocable break. They want to tear me down.
And now that Davis has been erased, a blank space
where memory stood, displayed in some stark museum,
I must concede, as I knew then, the poverty
of our cause. Slavery was our sin, and ours to find
redemption in. I could not command an army
against my kin, and so condemned myself to this
uplifted state of moral ambiguity.

Look at me. My sword is sheathed. I stare past you all
to a time before Sumter, before the Devil's
Choice. My feelings for my country were as ardent
and *unabated* as if still a green cadet
at West Point. Like Sam Houston, I knew what secession
would cost. Without slavery's curse, I would have faded
into obscurity, another minor blue
officer forgotten on frontier's blunted edge.
Coyote, cacti, and endless streams of idle
dreamers, speculators, like the little man who
commissioned me here. He could afford to resist,
outflank the inevitable revelation.

Robert Edward Lee reporting for duty, sir.
Around and above me these oaks sway. The autumn
wind from up the hill tussles a student's uncombed
hair. He remembers the holy promise that Truth
will set us free. He stares at me in shifting light,
verdigris, streaked in pollen, stained in grackle scat,
and ponders why I'm still here. I'm not a hero
for someone's lost cause. Take me down. Let truth march on.

KEN HADA, professor at East Central University in Ada, Oklahoma, has contributed to regional and national journals in the areas of ecocriticism, modern American, regional and ethnic literatures. In addition to his scholarly work, his eleventh book of poems, *Come Before Winter* (Turning Plow Press, 2023), was recently released. His poetry collection, *Contour Feathers* (Turning Plow Press, 2021), received the Oklahoma Book Award for poetry. Hada's poetry has been recognized and awarded by the Oklahoma Center for the Book, the National Western Heritage Museum, Western Writers of America, South Central Modern Language Association, and *The Writer's Almanac*. More at kenhada.org.

Buffalo River

I have seen the killing force
of this river—it rises fast
and furious—nothing
can survive its flooded torrent.

I have seen it in dry September
when pools of green
recoil into themselves,
when portage is required.

I have seen its cavernous source
springing into daylight,
its upper flows, its depth
through limestone bluffs

where hawks and eagles rest,
where hickory, cedar
and sycamore cling—oak
and walnut firm in the bottoms.

I have slept under magnetic stars
on her sandy beds
after paddling all day,
soul-searching in the sagacious sun

while songbirds provide chorus,
the rhythm certain—
my mind clearing in rapids
washing mottled gravel,

the line between life and death,
thin as a canoe bottom.
Autumn clouds gather
with the tired joy of rowing home.

Casting into Sunrise

The kayak sits still except for ripples
stirred when he arches the rod
back to a stop—then launches line
forward above unseeable water,

the sun's glare reflected on the glassy
surface before him, to some
spot where fish have splashed,
rising from midnight depth

leaving imagined wakes in water
for a target—both fisherman
and fish awakening to the same
old newness felt in flesh muscling

under sun—careful, quiet sounds
of intent—gentle for all its energy.

Morning Birds

In darkest light they sing with anticipation.

What Yo-Yo Ma does with his cello,
what the old painters did with their brush
cannot compare with their singing.

What I hear conjures feelings unnamed.

To live before sunrise is a gift I treasure.
To hear the first notes in darkness
fathers *and* mothers me—but then

I am left to listen, leaning into life.

I am both nurtured and orphaned
on this prairie hillside when light seems
so far off, but resounds so close—

my bones tremble like a tuning fork.

This is as close as I come to understanding
the distance between me and deity.
Even Mozart could never replace elements

that shape sounds in the dark—singular,
simple—a chorus that causes sunlight
to emerge blushing with glee.

Even Cedars

have their place,
an aggravating charm.
Disparaged as fireballs

as a nuisance to grass
and more attractive foliage,
they cover the fields

making homes for hidden birds,
providing berries for deer
in winter, and juncos

in January cold.
Their web-like leaves
holding soft snow

glisten in morning sun
after rain, unbowed
by frost or ice.

They line the fences—
a fortress of green
where quail and cottontails

take cover—the landscape
colored with their persistence,
with their stubborn refusal

to die, their lingering promise
to stay green in a world
littered with darkness.

Norvel Spring

The hotter the day the colder
the water tasted—most
used the communal gourd

dipped and sipped—
I flopped on my belly,
face down in the stone-stacked

structure framing the rising
translucent stream,
holding it still a moment

before it seeped downstream,
trickling like notes
played on Pan's flute—

a herd of bell-collared goats
on the hillside above
water cress and mint lining

its flow—a weeping willow
and a log cabin where an old man
kept Time at bay.

Born in Columbia, South Carolina, **TERRANCE HAYES** earned a BA at Coker College and an MFA at the University of Pittsburgh. In his poems, in which he occasionally invents formal constraints, Hayes considers themes of popular culture, race, music, and masculinity. Hayes's poetry collections include *So to Speak* (2023); *America Sonnets for My Past and Future Assassin* (2018), finalist for the National Book Award; *How to Be Drawn* (2015), finalist for the National Book Award and the National Books Critics Circle Award; *Lighthead* (2010), winner of the National Book Award and finalist for a National Book Critics Circle Award; *Wind in a Box* (2006), finalist for the Hurston-Wright Legacy Award; *Hip Logic* (2002), chosen for the National Poetry Series and finalist for an LA Times Book Award and an Academy of American Poets James Laughlin Award; and *Muscular Music* (1999), winner of a Kate Tufts Discovery Award. His poems have also been featured in several editions of Best American Poetry and have won multiple Pushcart Prizes. He is also the author of a prose book based on his Bagley Wright lectures: *To Float in the Space Between: A Life and Work in Conversation with the Life and Work of Etheridge Knight* (Wave Books, 2018), which was winner of the Poetry Foundation's 2019 Pegasus Award in Poetry Criticism, and of *Watch Your Language*, a collection of drawings and essays (Penguin, 2023). Hayes's additional honors include a Whiting Writers' Award and fellowships from the MacArthur Foundation, the National Endowment for the Arts, and the Guggenheim Foundation. He has taught at Carnegie Mellon University, the University of Alabama, and the University of Pittsburgh. Hayes is currently Professor of English at New York University.

Acknowledgments

"American Sonnet"
    First published in *Poetry*
"Pseudacris Crucifer"
    First published in *The New Yorker*
"Blackbird," "Buy One, Get One," and "Shafro"
    First published in *Muscular Music* (Carnegie Mellon
    University Press, 2006)

American Sonnet for My Past and Future Assassin
["Probably twilight makes Blackness dangerous"]

Probably twilight makes blackness dangerous
Darkness. Probably all my encounters
Are existential jambalaya. Which is to say,
A nigga can survive. Something happened
In Sanford, something happened in Ferguson
And Brooklyn & Charleston, something happened
In Chicago & Cleveland & Baltimore & happens
Almost everywhere in this country every day.
Probably someone is prey in all of our encounters.
You won't admit it. The names alive are like the names
In graves. Probably twilight makes blackness
Darkness. And a gate. Probably the dark blue skin
Of a black man matches the dark blue skin
Of his son the way one twilight matches another.

Pseudacris Crucifer

The father begins to make the sound a tree frog makes
When he comes with his son & daughter to a pail
Of tree frogs for sale in a Deep South flea market
Just before the last blood of dusk.
A tree frog is called a tree frog because it chirps
Like a bird in a tree, he tells his daughter
While her little brother, barely four years old,
Busies himself like a small blues piper
With a brand-new birthday harmonica.
A single tree frog can sound like a sleigh bell,
The father says. Several can sound like a choir
Of crickets. Once in high school, as I dissected
A frog, the frog opened its eyes to judge
Its deconstruction, its disassembly,
My scooping & poking at its soul.
And the little girl's eyes go wide as a tree frog's eyes.
Some call it the "spring peeper." In Latin
It's called *Pseudacris crucifer*. False locusts,
Toads with falsettos, their chimes issuing below
The low leaves & petals. The harmonica playing
Is so otherworldly, the boy blows with his eyes closed.
Some tree-frog species spend most every day underground.
They don't know what sunlight does at dusk.
They are nocturnal insectivores. No bigger than
A green thumb, they are the first frogs to call
In the spring. They may sound like crickets
Only because they eat so many crickets.
Tree frogs mostly sound like birds.
The tree frog overcomes its fear of birds by singing.
The harmonica playing is so bewitching,
The boy gathers a crowd in a flea market
In the Deep South. A bird may eat a frog.
A fox may eat the bird. A wolf may eat the fox.
And the wolf then may carry varieties of music
And cunning in its belly as it roams the countryside.

A wolf hungers because it cannot feel the good
In its body. The people clap & gather round
With fangs & smiles. The father lifts the son
To his shoulders so the boy's harmonics hover
Over varieties of affections, varieties of bodies
With their backs to a firmament burning & opening.
You can find damn near anything in a flea market:
Pets, weapons, flags, farm-fresh as well as farm-spoiled
Fruits & vegetables, varieties of old wardrobes,
A rusty old tin box with old postcards & old photos
Of lynchings dusted in the rust of the box.
You can feel it on the tips of your fingers,
This rust, which is almost as brown as the father
And the boy on his shoulders & the girl making
The sound a tree frog makes in a flea market
In the Deep South before the blood of dusk,
Just before the last blood of dusk. Just before the dusk.

Blackbird
(Calling My Brother to Hear Roberta)

She was the blackbird in our house,
Full of color and song like that.

My mother asleep on the couch,
My brother at his books,

I'd lock the bedroom door
To hear her Siren songs,

Let our music loop the room,
Flutter against the walls all night.

And I wanted a woman to someday
Make me feel like that,

Something better than orgasm or God,
Deeper than spoken words.

I wished for a woman's shoes
Tipped like blackbirds beside my bed,

Her bra, soft halves of a blackbird shell.
I wished for a woman's blackbird scent

And her blackbird touch beside my own.
I wished to always be in love.

Tonight, Roberta sings
Across nine hours of telephone lines,

And when I close my eyes, my mouth
Flings open like a June window.

In this empty room her song unlocks
The wing of my silent tongue.

Buy One, Get One

The old white man reading a box of *Corn Flakes* is like me.
Do you ever get up to go no where at sunrise? I shop at dawn
before all the good eggs are cracked. Only I & the elderly
know the supermarket is last vestige of America—
name brands & generic condiments, blackeye peas, white rice,
Spanish onions—everything has its cost. This morning
it's *Aint Jemima's Authentic Maple Syrup With Artificial Flavoring*,
BUY 1, GET 1 FREE. Meaning, one's half as much as usual
& I'm getting something for nothing. The cashier
has two buoyant breasts to compensate for her lack
of arithmetic. She hands me my change one coin at a time
as if I can't count. How much do I deserve?
In the 10th grade I knew briefly numbers to be the Grand
Daddies of the Cosmos. Pythagoras & Plato, knew it too—
MATH: realm of the Real & Infinite Truth. Each old man
was right to scorn poets for their noise about Death
& personal Beauty. Anyone will tell you, Poetry
is beautiful, but it ain't no super Model. Greeks had Logic
to compensate for their lack of Romance. Still, the Supermarket
with her aisles of cubes & cylinders & $3.14 cent pies
dons a kind of elegiac splendor. One plus one can equal one,
because, BUY 1, GET 1 FREE, means: 1 is Indivisible—
One Nation, with Liberty & Justice etcetera.
"Buy one, get one free," said the slave trader to cotton heads
when pregnant African girls mounted the auction block. America!
Everything has its price; nearly everything has been bought.

Shafro

Now that my afro's as big as Shaft's
I feel a little better about myself.
How it warms my bullet-head in Winter,

black halo, frizzy hat of hair.
Shaft knew what a crown his was,
an orb compared to the bush

on the woman sleeping next to him.
(There was always a woman
sleeping next to him. I keep thinking,

If I'd only talk to strangers . . .
grow a more perfect head of hair.)
His afro was a crown.

Bullet after barreling bullet,
fistfights & car chases,
three movies & a brief TV series,

never one muffled strand,
never dampened by sweat—
I sweat in even the least heroic of situations.

I'm sure you won't believe this,
But if a policeman walks up behind me, I tremble:
What would Shaft do? What would Shaft do?

Bits of my courage flake away like dandruff.
I'm sweating even as I tell you this,
I'm not cool,

I keep the real me tucked beneath a wig,
I'm a small American frog.
I grow beautiful as the theatre dims.

SILAS HOUSE is the *New York Times* bestselling author of seven novels, including *Lark Ascending* (Algonquin Books, 2022), which was a *Booklist* Editors' Choice and the winner of the 2023 Southern Book Prize; *Same Sun Here* (Candlewick, 2012); *Something's Rising: Appalachians Fighting Mountaintop Removal* (University Press of Kentucky, 2011), coauthored with Jason Kyle Howard; *Southernmost* (Algonquin Books, 2018); *Eli the Good* (Candlewick Press, 2010); *The Coal Tattoo* (Blair, 2005); *A Parchment of Leaves* (Ballantine Books, 2003); and *Clay's Quilt* (Blair, 2001). House is the recipient of three honorary degrees and other honors, including an E. B. White Award, the Lee Smith Award, the Caritas Medal, the Hobson Medal, and the Duggins Prize. In 2015, he was invited to read at the Library of Congress. House is a member of the Fellowship of Southern Writers and a former commentator on NPR's *All Things Considered*. He is the executive producer and one of the subjects of the documentary *Hillbilly*, winner of the L.A. Film Festival's Documentary Prize and the Foreign Press Association's Media Award. In 2024 House became a Grammy finalist for his work as a writer, creative director, and producer of the Tyler Childers music video "In Your Love." His novel *Southernmost* is currently in pre-production as a feature film. House teaches at Berea College, where he is the National Endowment for the Humanities Chair, and at the Naslund-Mann Graduate School of Writing. A native of Eastern Kentucky, House serves as Kentucky's poet laureate through 2025 and lives in Lexington, Kentucky.

Acknowledgments

"Cumberland Falls"
First published in *The Bitter Southerner*
"Rivers"
First published in *Still: The Journal*

Cumberland Falls

O, let them be . . .
     —Gerard Manley Hopkins

In high school the biggest dare was to slink
over the slick rocks flanking Cumberland Falls,
where the wide but shallow river dives
seventy feet into a deep pool of froth.
There, people say, catfish big as men twist
and slither, awaiting suppers sped
their way. You can see a rainbow at night,
shimmering on the mist during a full
moon and a clear sky. This is true. I snuck
behind the green curtain once with my best
friend, whose name I won't say because he
never came out. Just as we reached the veil
of water where we would disappear
into another world, I slipped. My right
leg slid down the cold boulder and before
I could plunge into the churning chaos
where torrent met river, he grabbed hold
of my hand. I was so electrified
by his touch I didn't think of how close
I was to being swept away.
Instead I thought how a small moment
of ecstasy is akin to drowning.
He held on for a beat longer
than necessary. He said something
I couldn't hear. I recall that often,
picturing his shiny lips, wondering
why I never asked him to repeat
himself later. The roar behind the falls
was a deafening symphony heard
only by those brave enough
to penetrate this darksome cavern
carved by centuries. Fern-laden, alive
with the smell of moss. A secret cathedral

made of wildness and wet. We were mesmerized,
and stood watching the falls as if frozen
yet, as if we might see through to the other side.

Little Fire

I was always so afraid of being left
behind. I was sure the Rapture would take
you all in the Twinkling of an Eye and strand
me. Because I questioned too much. Sometimes
I doubted. Often I pined for the lost boys
who sat petulant, aflame on the back pew.
One day the wrath was too much so I escaped.
I wandered for years, an Israelite
in the wilderness. Not one of you offered
shelter. I stood on your creaking porches
with a suitcase at my feet, staring at the closed
doors. I heard the clocks striking seven inside.
You watched from the curtain's edge, holding your breath.
I had nothing but little creeks and trees
to comfort me. Dogs, books, music, mountains. I
found a family when blood left me in the cold
night, but somehow, I kept myself warm.
All my life you've told me I'm no good. You've said
I am not worthy of God's love. But there was always this little fire
burning in me, and no one ever could put it out.

Rivers

(for Breonna Taylor)

Not far from the water
your daughter was sleeping.

O Kentucky: you hurt me and you heal me.
You cut me and you stitch me.

Your mountain tongues, your bluegrass
tongues, your western tongue,
your Louisville tongues.

Lou uh vuhl
Louey ville
Louis ville
Lou uh vuhl

On the banks of the Ohio.
The Cumberland and the Laurel.
Red River, Green River, Big
Sandy, Russell Fork, Levisa
Fork. And then:
the twisting Kentucky River.

O my Kentucky. You
hurt me and you heal me.
You cut me and you cut me.

Not far from the water
your daughter was sleeping.

When you won't listen you won't
listen. When you holler and scream.
When your silence means everything.

You hurt me. You cut me
and I wish you loved me
as much as I love you. I would
not just stitch you. I would never
cut you to begin with.

But then you march in the streets
for her. Then you say her name.
Then you lay down in front
of bulldozers. Then you stand
up for your children. And you
take me in, again. Begin
again. You put your arms around
me and tell me you love me.
You show me when you stitch me,
your needle catching the light
of the blue moon, the thread
that runs so true, the salve
made of coal, and tobacco, whiskey.
The salve made of rivers.

Not far from the water
Your daughter was sleeping.

Prove it, right now. Love me
as much as I love you.
She was a Kentuckian,
so be the best of Kentucky.
Be the holiness of your waters,
holy still even when polluted,
even when secret, when wild,
when dammed, in the dark stillness
of the night when you can hear
them if you hush, and listen.

ELLEN E. HYATT recalls her impetus for writing was becoming a Fellow of the Western Pennsylvania Writing Project (University of Pittsburgh) while teaching English. Later, teaching in Memphis, she learned her poetry was accepted for the Project's celebratory *Writing on the Desk*. Since living in Summerville, Hyatt has taught for English/communications departments; organized writing groups; and read in places as diverse as Charleston pulpits, Woodstock coffeehouses, and Beaufort bars—where rain leaked on manuscripts. When University of South Carilina's Poetry Initiative was active, Kwame Dawes selected Hyatt's poetry to be featured as an online chapbook. Other poems found homes in *Down the River*; *A Millennial Sampler of SC Poetry*; *Kakalak*; *Seeking* (inspired by Jonathan Green's art); and as recipients of SC's Poetry Society awards. Respecting organizations promoting arts and literacy, Hyatt's "village poet" for *Azalea Magazine* and a Life Member on the Board of Governors of SC's Academy of Authors.

Acknowledgments

"Winter by the Sea"
        First appeared in *Azalea Magazine*

Winter by the Sea

So this is another way you return:
as a warming memory of a winter's night
at an inn on the Carolina coast. We cannot
predict what will stir up the past, can we?
Or how long the image will last. Tonight,
a silver ladle dipped in a party punch bowl
ripples the surface in small waves, much like
actual larger ones rushing in and rolling out
until the sea becomes safely settled, soulful,
smooth. Smooth as the free sky is for gazing.

Stars that night seemed purposely placed.
Constellations ready for me and you to view.
With care, we strolled the shore until finding
drier sand, away from the tide line. There,
we laid down blanket, feather pillows,
and ourselves. Always prepared, you carried
a map of the night sky and a tiny flashlight
with a red filter. You said it helps eyes to get
adjusted before searching the wonder above us.
We were looking for a wide-open star cluster.

The stars felt familiar: depicted often in poems,
in paintings, in folklore, and in Greek myths
(ah . . . those never-ending tales to explain
creation, resulting in nothing but jealous rages
among gods). Within the cluster, we saw seven stars.
You pointed them out as Ursa Major or Big Dipper,
the ladle in the sky. Stars do appear as sweet surprise,
like bits of memory and other fragile beauty. Once
you warned me not to look too often or stay too long
because it might all just turn into another Paradise
lost.

Summer Night in the City

No escape—90 again. Air, puckers.
You feel trapped in the creases.
Loud odors, like those dying lilies
in hot little Southern churches, smother.
Sleepless,
you decide to move some bedding
to the fire escape's party balcony outside
your apartment window because
the AC's broken, and the Super's
drinking again.

As you try cooling off with images—
swimming at the base of Fairy Falls
out West; GQ's guy unbothered
in khakis and forever-crisp white shirt,
no matter the time or place; June Christy's
"Something Cool"—
a newer reality of cool arrives.

From somewhere floors above you,
someone else is also trying to forget.
A bass player. Flexible, his style
carries you away from the heavy heat.
The tone is mellow and leisured.
Unhurried notes fall lightly upon you
like rain upon new lovers.
They wait beneath a basswood,
the Linden,
not wanting this soft raining to end.

Seasonal Quartet

I. *The Arrival*

With birdsong and sky
looking like a package
wrapped in blue, tied
with white wispy ribbons,
March arrived—Oh, and
with a spring shower
of snow flowers.

II. *Multiplicity*

Strawberries
    no longer white with flower
        float ripe-red in cream.

III. *Somewhere, When Summer Joins Autumn*

A screen door blows shut;
An attic floor creaks;
And a purposeful, crisp click
of a small trunk latch
catches the yellow bow
on a straw hat.

IV. *Eve of the Newest Year*

He, on this threshold, believing
all he has left is a handful of frayed
calendared ideas from his pasts
. . . and regret . . .
to carry into a future,
could ask Janus what *he* would do
Now.

Light (a prose poem)

What is that light they see? Those who've been near death report to the living, "There was a tunnel. Then, I saw a bright light." Is it presumptive to think the light is of the First Day—His creative design? Or pillar of fire leading or garments of transfiguration? What if the light is from the sun of Day Four? Would we fear it now with all the warnings? Such quandaries we'll face. Shall we run toward or away? Could we make requests in our living wills: Lamplight, beacon, starlight, candlelight, porch light, or headlight? Campfire light, flashlight, spotlight, Tiki torch, neon, or vintage Edison? Let's choose moonlight. Just enough to read by and shawl our shoulders. Let the night be young. Let the words be yours once written to me on Maui's Lahaina shore.

After Seeing Kahaluʻu Grass Sprouting on Our Family Plot

"Whad'ya get?"
This, from one of the cottages
on Kamakoi Way where a woman
peeks at us from behind her door.
"Did you take a lot? Ooh la la."
She giggles and closes her door.
She does this each day we pack
belongings of another who's left.

How much do we really want
from the dead as we mourn?
Maybe their secret ingredient
in coconut cake? To hear
their island song in the queen conch
on their bookshelf? A favorite book?
I hold one. Its red cover, worn
and separating from the pages.
Sonnets from the Portuguese.
Sonnet V is dog-eared. There—
What a great heap of grief.

Wouldn't we be satisfied to learn
How to help heal heavy hearts?
How not to be sore losers to fate?
How to travel all the way *Through
ashen grayness*? And wouldn't we
want to find out—once and for all—
whether or not the grass
really is greener on the Other Side?

LUISA A. IGLORIA is the author of *Caulbearer* (Immigrant Writing Series Prize, Black Lawrence Press, 2024), *Maps for Migrants and Ghosts* (Co-Winner, 2019 Crab Orchard Open Poetry Prize), *The Buddha Wonders if She Is Having a Mid-Life Crisis* (2018), twelve other books, and four chapbooks. Originally from Baguio City, she makes her home in Norfolk, VA, where she is the Louis I. Jaffe and University Professor of English and Creative Writing at Old Dominion University's MFA Creative Writing Program. She also leads workshops for and is a member of the board of The Muse Writers Center in Norfolk. Igloria is the 20th Poet Laureate of the Commonwealth of Virginia (2020-22), Emerita. During her term, the Academy of American Poets awarded her a 2021 Poet Laureate Fellowship. Website: www.luisaigloria.com.

A Commonwealth

The common weal, meaning the body
     politic, the well-being of an entity or state.

The state capital, a Sunday in spring: streets
     where, even late in this century, I don't

see too many with my same face. Perhaps
     transients and students are gone on break.

Perhaps, dark-skinned ones like me are careful
     to avoid spaces where rebel flags with seven

stars still whip high in the wind, shameless
     declaration and misplaced belief that all men

are not created equal. But surely you've walked
     past the homeless on the avenue, stopped to listen

to buskers at the train station *take a sad song*
     and make it better, through chipped teeth and smiles.

Commencement Day

Yesterday the streets were filled with slow-
moving traffic. It inched up the boulevard,

snaked around the side of the stadium,
clogged the entrances to our quiet

residential streets. Streams of people
headed into the labyrinth of ceremony—

this one called commencement, which means
both the end and the beginning. Whoever

makes speeches invoking sacrifice
and the future or that ubiquitous word

journey while covering up their own
corruption, should just shut up.

Let the trees give the valedictory
and the billows confer their tasseled caps.

Let the noon heat gild the heads of those
who've labored bravely, even with no prior

guarantee of reward. Let the procession
of bodies shimmer like a promise

that kindness and comradeship will keep
rising up like wild flowers in the fields.

What We Want

My friend, who's recently become a parent, is venting
again about the ways working moms are so unnoticed

and undercompensated, if at all. Her LinkedIn profile
has descriptors like results-oriented and self-starter;

public policy analyst, program director. She owns
and can actually pull off wearing a fancy gold-colored

jumpsuit; she leads a nonprofit organization and hops
on planes to attend conferences out of state but

I know too well that kind of physical, mental, and emotional
exhaustion though we might have gentle, supportive

partners, and a freezer drawer packed with microwavable
meatballs or emergency dumplings. After I delivered

(such an easy-sounding word, like something one does
with takeout pizza or wings plus extra fries) my last

child, groggy and sleep-deprived, I went back to work
after only ten days, since I had no maternity leave benefits.

Lecturing on critical analysis and *Woman Warrior* before
a roomful of mostly bored students, I'd feel my milk-

engorged breasts leak underneath my blazer and flush
from embarrassment—but mostly from the fear

I'd be reduced to just a body that did whatever things
a body did before pushing another body into the world.

I do but also don't want to tell my friend that it all gets
easier somewhere down the line—untruth that rolls off

each page of books with titles like *On Becoming a Woman*
or *The Housewife's Guide to Becoming Wealthy*, their slick

covers depicting their impeccable houses and impossibly
narrow, postpartum waists. But I do want to say, this has not

and never has been a country of easy, whichever way
we look at it. There are parts of me that want to answer

an ad for caretaker of a remote island between the West
Coast of Scotland and the Isle of Skye, and parts

that want to stay writing in a coffee shop, until
the baristas kick me out. Parts of me want

to scream and scold or throw pots at a tiled
wall; and parts of me will sob, wring their hands

and want to die but not do it after all though life,
as we know, is so hard and people so heartless;

but tomorrow is Wednesday and there's a farmer's
market where one can get the crunchiest peas

and fresh strawberries. I want to make something good
from that, and just watch the people I love eat it, the way

my mother would stand at the kitchen door watching me clean
my plate after school, eyes puffy after a good cry of her own.

Grief Landscape

When Helios' son is felled by a lightning bolt, the seven
sisters of Phaethon grieve for months. Out of their tears
comes amber; they themselves are turned into poplar
trees. Deserts are scorched into being, and mountains
shaped as if by earth-movers. The landscapes of grief
are ragged with untrimmed grass and sharp with
boulders; they're rimmed with the stars' metallic
shine. Pigeons roosting in the eaves have feathered
breasts the shade of sudden bruises, the shape
of hearts if you could hold them whole in your hands.

Yesterday I walked
through a winding hallway lit
with others' unseen breaths.

Exit Essay, Asian American Lit.
(with lines from Langston Hughes)

The student wrote in her assessment
that she learned *Asian Americans*
have evolved from being the filthiest
to the smartest people. I guess
she was thinking of the model minority,
but somehow thought the stereotype
a developmental endpoint, after viewing
slides depicting how xenophobia is not new
(nor only from 2016), but has been around
for hundreds of years. "Yellow fever" scares
were in editorial cartoons and magazines
from the 1800s—In one, a rough-garbed
Chinaman is drawn with buck teeth, sinister
eyebrows, and a long queue whipping
behind him like a snake. He stands suggestively
astride a white woman prone on the ground,
torch in one hand and smoking pistol in the other.
25 years ago, after arriving in this city, I didn't
immediately realize why our landlord
would drop by with no warning,
and randomly mention that the previous
tenant kept the premises scrupulously clean—
though the week we moved in, I found
a greenish slime across the entire refrigerator
top. There have been students who refuse
to address me by my title, even colleagues
who've questioned my credentials. I used
to keep quiet and just let the micro-
aggressions slide, but not anymore.
Not anymore will they pass. I laugh,
and eat well, and grow strong.

ASHLEY M. JONES is the 2022-2026 poet laureate of Alabama. She is the first person of color and the youngest person to serve in this role in Alabama history. Jones is the author of three poetry collections: *REPARATIONS NOW!* (Hub City Press, 2021); *dark // thing* (Pleiades Press, 2019), winner of the Lena-Miles Wever Todd Prize for Poetry; and *Magic City Gospel* (Hub City Press, 2017), winner of the silver medal in poetry in the Independent Publisher Book Awards. Jones is coeditor of *WHAT THINGS COST: an anthology for the people* (University Press of Kentucky, 2023). Her poems and essays appear or are forthcoming in journals and anthologies that include the Academy of American Poets, *Poetry* magazine, *Tupelo Quarterly*, *Hand in Hand: Poets Respond to Race*, and the *Harvard Journal of African American Policy*. She has been featured by CNN and the BBC, on *Good Morning America*, in the *New York Times*, and on ABC News.

Acknowledgments

"Eating Red Dirt in Greensboro, Alabama," "God Speaks to Alabama," "Viewing a KKK Uniform at the Civil Rights Institute," and "Birmingham Fire and Rescue Haiku"
    First appeared in *Magic City Gospel*
"On My Way to the Edmund Pettus Bridge, I Think of My Father"
    First appeared in *The Forum by Phi Kappa Phi*

Eating Red Dirt in Greensboro, Alabama

I ate red dirt for the first time
with Aunt Hattie—big, brown blind angel
who listened to local crimes

on her police scanner. Its monotone lullaby
crooned all through the night, piercing, faithful.
When she heard it was my first time,

she sent us to the hill. We scraped it off, tried
to ignore the ants and the strange, dull
sour scent. Stealing dirt, a local crime,

only punished by whatever was hiding inside
our Ziploc bags: a pillbug, a ladybug's broken shell.
Back from the hunt, for the first time

I realized how citified
I really was, scared of something so full
of local germs. But was it a crime

to fear eating dirt? Finally, my Southern pride
made me put it to my lips, resist the acidic pull
of bile in my throat. And for the first time,
I felt like a local, swallowing this bittersweet crime.

God Speaks to Alabama

I molded you
from red clay, sweet cornbread,
the slow drip of a lemon
squeezed over sugar and ice.
I kissed you to life, on the lips.
mama bird I am—
my tongue feeds you blood.
I have waited
in this heat for you
to pucker
and say my name—
Hallelujah, Alabama.
I give you fire
and blackberries
and white, thick cotton.
I give you the honeybee
and the yellowhammer—
find me, swallow me down
and whisper me
to passersby
as you sit, nightly,
on the creaky
front porch.

Viewing a KKK Uniform at the Civil Rights Institute

All you can really tell at first
is that it was starched.
Some Betty Sue, Marge, Jane,
some proper girl
with a great black iron
made those corners sharp.
The hood, white and ablaze
with creases,
body flat and open
for husband, brother, son.
Behind the glass,
it seems frozen, waiting
for summer night
to melt it into action,
for the clean white flame
of God to awaken its limbs.
In front of it, you are dwarfed—
you imagine a pair of pupils
behind the empty holes
of the mask.
Behind the stiff cotton,
would the eyes squint
to see through small white slits,
or would they open wide
as a burning house
to hunt you down
until you pooled
like old rope
before them?

Birmingham Fire and Rescue Haiku, 1963

What about us said
we were on fire? What said
extinguish quickly,

fill up the hose and
set the dogs loose? Could they smell
our confusion? Or

was it our singing?
Were our voices like sirens,
a chorus of blood?

We were wet black seeds
in that raw Birmingham flesh—
we germinated.

Did the photos show
our fingers stretching like roots?
Did they show our eyes,

how they reached sunward,
to the hot, bright, silent star
that could turn water

to steam, seeds to fruit?
Did they see themselves become
our fertilizer?

On My Way to the Edmund Pettus Bridge, I Think of My Father

I don't know when will be the last days
of my life. Today, on the road from Montgomery
to Selma, I can't help but think of death. Can't help
but hear its familiar quiet settling down on the bright
green land. There is something in the memory
of protest called fear. Still. I feel it when I remember
the way some men beat the soft pulp
of the marchers' bodies until it was a paste.
I remember the way my skin signifies, sometimes,
chains and the necessity of force. Of death.

Any day could be my last.

I don't know who will be there when it's my time to go,
whether by nature or by force. I wonder
if my father knew it was coming when he died,
if he had a moment to see the sky before
it went black. If he smelled the sweetness
of the breeze as it passed him. I hope he thought of me,
of all of us. I hope he wished us well.
I hope his mother greeted him in heaven,
open arms made of angel wings.

I hope, when it's my time to go, I see him
in an unending garden in the sky,
tending a patch of collards ready to be plucked.
I hope he turns to me with soil on his fingers
and that thinking furrow on his brow.
Maybe, as I leave this earthly realm he'll ask me to help
him pick some greens like we did one Thanksgiving
a lifetime ago. I hope I feel the grip of their green hands.
Their veins full as my soul.

JOHN LANE is the author of many books of poetry and prose. He has won the Louisville Review Poetry Prize and Prairie Schooner's Glenna Luschei Award. His *Abandoned Quarry: New & Selected Poems* won the SIBA (Southeastern Independent Booksellers Alliance) Poetry Book of the Year prize in 2012. A co-founder of the Hub City Writers Project in Spartanburg, SC, Lane also taught creative writing and environmental studies at Wofford College for over three decades. In 2014 he was inducted into the SC Academy of Authors and his literary papers are part of the Sowell Family Collection in Literature, Community and the Natural World at Texas Tech University.

Sweet Tea

God rested on the seventh day, but early in the morning,
    before the sun strained into the southern sky,
    she made sweet tea from scratch. She boiled the water
    in a black kettle, put in the orange pekoe bags
    and let them stand as the water perked, and then
    she did what gods know to do: she heaped in Dixie
    Crystal sugar while the brew was still warm as the day.

For God so loved the world she made sweet tea. For she served
    the tea to anyone who admired her creation. To anyone
    walking down the street of the wet new neighborhood,
    to the mail man delivering early on that next day
    of that second week, to the milk man in his truck, to the black
    man working in the yard, to the white man selling peaches
    door-to-door. On God's sidewalk there was an X scratched
    by hobos. They knew come to God's back door and you'd
    get a plate of leftovers and all the sweet tea you could drink.
    They knew the sugared pints of contentment. They drank sweet
    tea from God's back steps and went on their wandering way again.

For God knows sweet tea fills with love and refreshment from
    any long train. For sweet tea is safe as an oak forest
    camp. Sweet tea, clinks in jelly jars. Sweet tea,
    sweeter as it stands. For God's sake we brew it
    like religion. For God's sake we carry it now in Styrofoam
    cups in cars. We drink it in winter. We drink it always.

And this poem would not lessen sweet tea's place in the creation.
    Sweet tea is not fading from the southern towns like the Confederate
        flag,
    lives in houses all over town. Black folk brew it often as white folk.
    Take the flag off the state capitol. It doesn't mean anything to me,
    but leave me my sweet tea. This poem stands as a recipe for being
        civil.

This poem stands cold sweet tea up as God's chosen beverage.
  The manifest southern brew. When sad I draw figures in the
      condensation
  of glasses of sweet tea. I connect the grape leaves on the jelly jar.
  I cast out any restaurant that will not make it from scratch.
  When lonely for southern sweet tea I go to the house of my beloved.

For I love a woman who makes sweet tea late at night to eat with
      Chinese.
  For her hands move like God's through the ritual.
  For it is as if she had learned along with speaking in tongues.
  For I love the way her hands unwrap the tea bags and drop them in
      the water.

For I love the unmeasured sugar straight from the bag,
  the tap water from deep in the earth.
  For these processes are as basic to love as love making.
  Our bodies are both brown like suntans inside from years of tea.
  For sweet tea is the southern land we share, the town, the past.
  When we kiss it is sweet tea that we taste as our lips brush.
  For when we are hot it is sweet tea we crave.
  When we have children it will be sweet tea
  they learn along with Bible stories and baseball.

Elvis

I try to remember his voice rising
from the single speaker of the De Soto.
I was four in 1958 when Elvis returned
from the Army, to Mama, Vernon, fame.

That was before the Fall, before the devil
placed a gilded sash in Elvis's rockabilly hands
and opened the yellow dance hall curtain.

My childhood was cracked open too,
by the British Invasion. I lost so much
listening to the new pop from overseas.
Almost as much as Elvis lost to Graceland.

Yes, Elvis grew fat and Elvis took pills.
Elvis learned the price of a poor boy's success.
I grew my hair shaggy, took up air guitar
on a tennis racket, sang "Love, love me do."

It could it have been different. He could still
be alive, singing on the Americana
showcase, adding in a few old Jimmy Rogers
numbers, a deep-South Springsteen.

I could have found the Elvis inside
had that novel sold, had that script sent me
down the road on the Luck Bus. We could all
be Elvis and Elvis could be us too.

On That Old Habit of Not Paying Bills,
Though the Money Is in the Bank

When my check came I would act out like a man on hourly wages.
I celebrated the feast of abundance in all the quarters of my body.
I bought expensive beer, lots of it, took a bead on Saturday night,
counted the bills over one-by-one, citizen for a day in the City of Flush.
I'd come home from bar, pool hall, juke joint, patio, dive,
say a prayer to the host of folding money, empty my pockets on the
    dresser,
put a little aside for next week's lunch money, hide what was left.

You Who Would be Rich, this was the small still voice of the unsalaried.

Deed Book

Greene County, NC

Granted to me, Pole Cat Swamp
32 acres of piney woods land
the edge of the gum pocosin, near my joined fields
the mouth of a ditch, my dividing corner
the land where I now live deeded to me
the country road at the Poley Bridge and Wolf Pit Branch
on Howell Swamp

on the S side of Middle Swamp
on the S side of Sandy Run
on the N side of Wheat Swamp, in the fork of Gully Branch

Granted Beaver Dam Swamp, the new road, the run of Wheat Swamp
to say, one half of the seine place known
by the name of Black Fish Hole
Edwards Mill Pond on Tysons Marsh
the fork of the branch, east prong of sd. branch, the old mill corner
in Miller's patient
and the run of Gum Branch, opposite the dividing fence
the road adjacent to Rasberry
near the old brick kilns corner

Granted the Sandy Island field on the new road,
the W prong of the Wolf Pit swamp agreed upon at the mouth of a
    ditch . . .
Granted Jumping Run now called Mill Run,
mouth of the mill run including one half of the mill seat . . .
also, the run of Watery Branch where the ditch cut
by Blarney Baker empties into sd. branch, Jack's Branch,
the line of land, Maple Branch, a dividing stake between the Pate
land and Handy Hughes
Granted Sandy Run at the mouth of Hardy Branch, the old crossing
    place

in accordance of Elizabeth Whitley,
a lunatic, granted the pitch path, head of a small branch, down
to its mouth with Horse Pen Branch
the run of Cat Tail Swamp
a branch in a field near the crossing place
near Panthers Swamp

Granted to me the run of Nahunta
to me a path, a small branch, an agreed corner
an old road, opposite where the old chapel formally stood
on the road, Chappel Branch, where the county road
crosses same Toss Not Swamp, Poley Causeway Branch,
head of Dry Marsh, a ditch, Speight, Contentnea Creek,
mouth of Toss Not, near the Water Hole Pocosin
Thompson Swamp, Marsh Branch, and head of Pasture Branch

to me granted the public road, the foot of the old bridge
formally crossed Wheat Swamp
the S side of Rain Bow
Johnson's Branch, the Caswell path

Dudley Run Swamp, the great path granted
Britt Branch, Thompson Swamp, Bennetts field
formally known as Wilcox Land
the run of the swamp (say Wheat Swamp)
the middle of the marsh to Spring Branch,
the head of Laney Hole, Great Contentnea Creek,
the mouth of Nahunta Creek
Cowford Branch, White Oak Pocosin
Lane's Branch, three tracts on Button Branch
Fox Grape Branch, Light Wood Knot Swamp

Granted a small drain, E side of Jumping Run
Cat Tail Swamp
the run of Britt's Pocosin, the mouth of Horse Pen Branch
Pape's Dwindling Branch
Apple Tree Swamp, Hardee Branch, near the horse ford
the mouth of a 4-ft ditch opposite Jordan Whitley's field

lying in the fork of the swamp
new ground reserved
for the use of Mrs. Sidney Coward
with all necessary timber to keep up the fence
around sd. excepted field for her life and no longer

Meteorology: A Play in Six Scenes

I.
Last night the wind
Reversed course,
Spoiler in the season's
Latest pot boiler.
Trunks auditioned
As compasses,
Pointing true north.

II.
If Hamlet lived
His legacy as a tree
He would be sweet gum
Snapped, pointing
Two ways at once.

III.
Weather is a show
That never closes, casting,
Fluid as time.

IV.
And wind is a stage
Quickly struck.
Wind is an improv
Troupe leaving town.

V.
The acorn grows
An oak in its ear,
Then learns its lines.

VI.
No tragedy in the forest.
Even fire is a question

Flame asks of the future.
The pith of some doomed
Quercus has already lodged
In the stump's duff.

A professor of English at the University of South Carolina, **ED MADDEN** grew up on a rice and soybean farm in rural Arkansas. He is the author of six books of poetry, most recently *A pooka in Arkansas* (The Word Works, 2023). He served as the inaugural poet laureate for the City of Columbia, SC, 2015-2022. In 2019, he received a Poet Laureate Fellowship from the Academy of American Poets. He is recipient of artist residencies at the Hambidge Center for the Creative Arts in Georgia and the Instituto Sacatar in Itaparica, Brazil.

Postcards from Arkansas

What landscape do
you carry inside you?
Cut me open: soybean rows.
Cut me open: fields of rice.
My heart's a combine auger,
my spine the gravel road
I roamed with cousins.

◊◊◊

My aunt said that when she dies
she doesn't want the usual to-do—
pall-bearing nephews in dark suits.
No, not that, not black, she said.
She wants her casket carried out
by all her nieces, dressed in red.

◊◊◊

We pulled up nothing on the trot-line
that day but a gar, ridged and slick,
almost prehistoric, dead, probably
bigger in memory than it was.

◊◊◊

Take kaolin from a souvenir box
of Arkansas minerals and rocks.
Place it against your tongue,
this souvenir of where you're from.
It will stick. Now try to talk
with something from home
holding down your tongue.

Postcards from Hambidge

Rabun's Gap, Georgia

A tremble of pale green leaves
on the ground just beyond
the door of the studio. A breeze
shuffles them, then they lift—
wings. *A luna moth.*

◊◊◊

A small bird tsk-tsks
from the tall grass.

◊◊◊

At the end of the hike,
I dove into the creek.
The cold was a shock.
I swam across.
I swam back.

◊◊◊

The moon was too bright.
We held up our hands
as we lay back on the lawn—
our DIY eclipse to block its light.
As our eyes adjusted, the sky
deepened, thickened
with more stars, and more.

◊◊◊

The trees are full of eyes
and ears. The birds quiet

as I pass, pick up the song
when I've gone by.
The creek carries on.

◇◇◇

The composer takes a bird's song
and stretches it into long tones.
It is like a room full of violins.

◇◇◇

Because they are
so moved, the trees
applaud the wind.

◇◇◇

The moth-bit drapes of night
are drawn so quickly over the light.

◇◇◇

This morning the trees
have dressed up as trees, again.
Sometimes they have been
more like tall old men
quietly discussing the news.

◇◇◇

New ideas rarely
announce their arrival,
but sometimes your
head is on fire, and
wild things moving
through the trees.

◇◇◇

When our eyes meet,
a woodpecker slides
shy behind the tree.
The crow looks me
over for a moment,
goes back to tossing
leaves and moss.

◇◇◇

What I thought was solid ground
is not. What I thought was solid
ground is not. What I thought
was solid ground is not. What
I thought was solid ground is not.

◇◇◇

The artist says he is working with time
as we walk through the flood meadow,
another who is painting landscapes
here, *en plein air*, that she wants to find
something new in the old forms.
I wonder, are all landscapes elegies now?

Praise Song, June 2020

Praise the disease that killed the dogwood, praise
the dogwood that died, slowly. Praise chainsaw
and rope. Praise the truck that picks up
the yard debris, the man who tells us to cut it
smaller or they won't pick it up next time.
Praise the time it takes to cut and stack
the branches. Praise the branches, praise the roots
we'll never dig up. Praise gloves. Praise
the loppers, the shears, the different shapes of shovel—
who knew there were so many kinds of shovels?
Praise the shovels, praise the rake. Praise the good
wheelbarrow, the black one, and even praise
the broken one—it still rolls and works
well enough when my husband is using the other.

Praise the old hat that sometimes keeps
the sweat out of my eyes. Praise sweat,
praise the salt in my mouth, the sting in my eyes.
Praise dog fennel and thistle, wild onion and dock.
Praise smell and taste, praise basil and chives.
Praise the tangle of honeysuckle ripped from
the azaleas, but only after we've stripped
the blossoms to steep in boiling water. Praise
honeysuckle syrup, uriny yellow and grassy sweet.

Praise the acanthus surging in the sun, now
the dogwood's gone. Praise the light the dead
give. Praise the window filled with sky,
praise the new view, praise the old, the white
blossoms every spring till this, the red
leaves of late October, the red berries
that fed the birds. Praise the feasting birds.

Praise the cardinal glistening like a flower
in the camellia, now that the flowers have all
fallen. Praise the yellow fungus that has taken
the quince, the fruit garish now with rot.
Praise the porn show of orange stinkhorns
thrust up among the peppers and lettuce.
Praise the brown gardenias that still smell sweet.
Praise fester and stink, praise compost
and rot and that really foul fish
emulsion that won't burn the leaves when you
fertilize in the heat. Praise the heat.

Praise the bristling roadside blackberries, twining
with Virginia creeper, poison ivy. Praise the black
and red berries, praise the stains on our hands.
Praise the poison ivy its lessons: watch
where you step, where you put your hand.
Praise sunburn, praise ant bite. Praise
ants and praise the poison we sugar over
them, praise the way they boil up
when we kick the mounds. Praise the snake
that startled my husband as he moved rocks
he'd stacked up for another project, a king snake
like a coil of black and gold rope, and praise
the tiny legless lizards we found under
the rocks. Praise the rocks, for what they are,
and what they may yet be. Praise the yard
that keeps us busy, now, during the long
sheltering, that gives us things to do together.
Praise the long sheltering, for those who
can shelter, praise the shelter.

Stitches

Jan 1, 2022

On Wednesday, I had a skin cancer cut
from my back, just below my right
shoulder—not very poetic, I suppose,

that brown spot of *unusual cellular growth*,
as the doctor put it, when I lay down
on my stomach and what felt like a nest

of polite wasps took turns, stung me
numb and then the doctor excised some skin
to send off for tests and now there are

seven stitches there where something—
a wing maybe—might have grown.
On Thursday I met an old high school friend

on Zoom, someone I hadn't seen since
the ten-year reunion in 1991. He told me
about his gay uncle in New York and the friend

he lived with—*everyone knew but no one
said*—that generation, he said, when men
moved away, came home alone at Christmas,

left a partner in the city, what some still
expect, my brother saying a few years ago
that I am always welcome *but your friend,*

the man I've been with more than two decades
now, *is not.* Someday I expect he'll meet him,
the man who carefully pulled the bandage off

on Friday, New Year's Eve, helped me rinse
the wound, gently, in the shower, then
swabbed the skin with mupirocin ointment

and put a new bandage on the stitches
and we celebrated with homemade pizza, later
champagne, walked out into the dark street

at midnight to see what we could see, lights
exploding over the trees, and listened, all
around us the rolling thunder of starting over.

Vanishing

after Michael Moreno's "Childhood"

All those fields I mistook for home, rows of soybeans and milo and the smell of wellwater as we rode in the back of the pickup truck at dusk—

the windshield a thickening scum of dead bug—

those rows more like lessons on vanishing, all things converging somewhere in the future, that spot on the horizon, that border, that ditch.

Childhood was blister and itch,

was pokeberry ink and dirtclod wars, was toad pee and roadkill, was jumping off the porch to roll in the mounds of clover, the yard never mown till thick enough to choke the mower,

and the white blooming clover

trembling with bees, the yard riddled with ticks, and snakes in the grass—my mother was sure of it—and a rat snake climbing the screen door one summer, my mother calling my father,

repeating *kill it kill it kill it*—

CAMPBELL MCGRATH is the author of twelve books of poetry, including *XX: Poems for the Twentieth Century, Nouns & Verbs: New and Selected Poems*, and *Fever of Unknown Origin* (Knopf, 2023). He has received numerous literary prizes for his work, including the Kingsley Tufts Award, a Guggenheim Fellowship, a MacArthur Fellowship, a USA Knight Fellowship, and a Witter-Bynner Fellowship from the Library of Congress. His poetry has appeared in the *New Yorker, Harper's, Atlantic* and on the op-ed page of the *New York Times*, as well as in scores of literary reviews and quarterlies. Born in Chicago, he lives in Miami Beach and teaches at Florida International University, where he is the Philip and Patricia Frost Professor of Creative Writing and a Distinguished University Professor of English.

Ariel in Florida

I.

Before thought was born the dawn arrived—
the sun rose and that was the first idea,

shadows of coconut palms against sand, images
running away from the bodies that spawned them.

Mangrove root, cypress knee, scapula, polyp, frond.
Language of bones, archaeology of the umbilicus,

syntax, propagation, the unfurling
of the mist-loving tree fern, leaf by ancient leaf.

Before words, seeds: before songs, spells.
Before representation the things themselves.

At night the stars wheeled past, inventing mathematics,
and spiders learned to weave in their honor.

The full moon called the Atlantic to her side,
its waters grown salty with envious tears.

Before hymns to hydrogen and atomic geometries,
before pistil and stamen, before gnosis—the sun.

II.

Before the tempest, before Prospero's whirlwind,
they were alone together on their island,
Ariel and Caliban, rough creatures that they were.

Even after the storm he refused to leave
so she sailed west on a raft of Sargasso weed,
adorned in its bestiary of jewels and flagella,
washing ashore on a beach of chalk-white marl.

This was Florida, the real world, fully formed.
No more enchantments, no more primitive rapture.

So she became the spirit of the place,
strange as it was, mangrove pods for fingers,
anole eggs for eyes and conch shells for ears,
her footprints spinning small hurricanes of coral,

given entirely to the life that lay before her,
hour by hour, blessing by blessing, task by task—

to sleep exhausted at the pleasure of the waves,
to dream clothed only in amulets of moonlight,
to command eternity to echo within a lightning whelk,
to reign as golden as the tabebuia tree,
to praise above all things the sun and to love it
as it loves every flower that blossoms there,
tirelessly, deliriously, without thought of tomorrow.

The Everglades

Green and blue and white, it is a flag
for Florida stitched by hungry ibises.

It is a paradise of flocks, a cornucopia
of wind and grass and dark, slow waters.

Turtles bask in the last tatters of afternoon,
frogs perfect their symphony at dusk—

in its solitude we remember ourselves,
dimly, as creatures of mud and starlight.

Clouds and savannahs and horizons,
its emptiness is an antidote, its ink

illuminates the manuscript of the heart.
It is not ours though it is ours

to destroy or preserve, this the kingdom
of otter, kingfisher, alligator, heron.

If the sacred is a river within us, let it flow
like this, serene and magnificent, forever.

The Ladder

The past, a dust-covered shoebox recovered
from my mother's attic, does not open easily.

Webs of duct tape, the ladder one must climb
into the unfinished attic, hot as a coffin—

going up the light bulb shatters
against my skull and the shadows deepen.

But in the end it yields, and photographs spill
across the kitchen table like playing cards.

She in her beautiful wedding dress,
my father in the uniform of youth.

There I am, with a cap gun and cowboy hat
on Christmas morning some geologic age ago.

Further in, deeper down
to the antique black and white images,

yellow-margined, crimped with age,
backed with carefully penciled notes:

my grandmother beside the cottage in Donegal;
my grandfather, newly arrived in America,

on a New York City rooftop with two friends
nobody remembers the names of

Donegal—that green archaism—
and Manhattan in the 1930s, polyglot dynamo,

all that was great about the Twentieth Century
fermenting in its democratic casks.

And there, in a battered Irish tintype,
is my great-grandmother, Margaret McGuire.

I've never seen her before.
I've never even thought to imagine her.

Widowed young, turned away
by her husband's impoverished people,

with three daughters to raise
and only the needlework to keep them,

monogrammed handkerchiefs
and lace-edged linen tablecloths, a life

beyond my powers of narrative comprehension,
notations I cannot translate from ancient script.

Donegal derives from the Irish *Dún na nGall*,
Dún meaning fort or tower or castle,

and *nGall*, meaning foreigner, outlander, stranger,
in memory of the conquerors who occupied it.

The Castle of the Stranger.
Which is another name for the past.

At the Ruins of Miami Beach

Four days at sea we came upon rock formations in shallow water
which proved to be the remnants of an ancient metropolis,
long-collapsed towers become a nursery for enormous grouper,
avenues of corrosive rust scrawled with sponge-beds, eel grass,
wraith-like leopard rays ghosting wrecked causeways,
cyclones of yellowtail snapper, blue tang, black drum,
clouds of coral polyps dispersing like pollen on a tidal breeze
to construct amidst the ruins their fabulous condominiums.

Who were these long-forgotten folk? Why build such marvels
on a sandbar at the edge of a hurricane-haunted sea?
Of enterprise they possessed a plenty, of common sense a nullity.
The past is a riddle to match the enigma of human will.
Deep-sixing their relics, we weighed anchor, charted the debris,
and set sail in search of some less bewildering discovery.

On the Three Forms of Water

Ever since I learned about sea-level rise
I've been binge-watching the Atlantic Ocean
but nothing ever really happens. It goes up,
it goes down. Sometimes king tides
flood a section of the city, which is nice
for the street-sweepers and canoeists.

I am so used to thinking about myself
that it's hard to understand the sea.
What use is singularity in imagining that
seamless, quicksilver commonwealth?

The ocean is liquid, like the mind, elastic
tides of consciousness flowing and probing,
interrogating whatever seeks to contain it.

Ice is like the body, scarred and fractured,
ordained to crack, diminish, melt away.

And the third form—fog on a window,
ghostly mist, the clouds
which adorn the sky in celestial vestments
we glimpse as gaudy rags at sunset—
what could it be but the soul?

We are liquid and we are solid, oceanic
matter cloaked in the garment of being.

As for the ocean: she is coming to collect us
and gather us back into herself, as when,
long ago, your mother picked you up early
from the nurse's office at school,
and gave you a kiss, and put you to bed,
where you slept without a care in the world.

JIM MINICK is the author or editor of eight books, including *The Intimacy of Spoons* (poetry), *Without Warning: The Tornado of Udall, Kansas* (nonfiction), *Fire Is Your Water* (novel), and *The Blueberry Years: A Memoir of Farm and Family*. His work has appeared in many publications, including the *New York Times, Poets & Writers, Oxford American, Orion, Shenandoah, Appalachian Journal, Wind*, and *The Sun*. He serves as coeditor of *Pine Mountain Sand & Gravel* and lives in the mountains of Virginia.

Acknowledgments

"To Spoon"
        First appeared in *Upper New Review*

To Spoon

To spoon is not to fork—
that's what we do to steaks
and roads and manure.

To fork is to pierce, penetrate, puncture.
To fork is to split and branch,
to pay up and cough out,

but also to tune.
We forklift crates. We pitchfork hay.
The devil never carries a spoon.

Can you bang forks and get a song?

To spoon is not to knife—
that's what we do too often
to bodies and silence.

To knife is to slice,
to stab and wound,
to skin, filet, and butcher.

To knife is to dam
water that once
spooned the land.

Can you play knives without getting hurt?

Yet the tool is innocent:
a fork feeds or gigs;
a spoon ladles soup or cooks H—

and a knife? To scalp
and to scalpel
both require a sharp blade.

Listen to the drumming of the spoons.

To spoon is to slip into sleep
and the same soft, slow breath,

to listen to the rain
with one ear.

Coyote Grace

From low in her belly, a coyote lifts
her voice to ascend that organ pipe
of a throat to clarity of dusk
and cue for pups to join with yips and squeaks
that nurture the air to vibrate
with what seems like joy like ecstasy
of sound of the body an instrument
the larynx a box to strum with one long exhale—
this yodeling school for pups, choir
practice with only sopranos, for now,
and time to learn to listen to kin
on haunches nearby and a mile away:
this nightly hairy news with lips wide,
eyes bright, whiskers funneling the wind,
this town-square opera of hot breath,
hillside tail-curled revival—
O for a Thousand Tongues to Sing?—
jazzed with ostinatos and skat
for non-cats, fresh blood overture,
roadkill serenade, growling gratitude,
a thick-fur kind of grace, close
enough to hollow out your chest, close enough
to hear each voice, close enough to sing
along and then listen to the ache
of an echo long and slow and longer still.

It ends as sudden as it starts,
no benediction, no amen,
unless the whole song is one long
amen to this holy, falling dark.

            And then we eat.

Gas

*for the boat-tailed grackles at Love's Truck Stop off I-95
near Brunswick, GA, and for the woman on the bench in
Jacksonville, FL*

The boat-tailed grackle golden-eyes me
from the #8. He puffs his throat,
raises his crown, rudders his black tail.
Below, the magic mouth quick kisses
my credit card (petro-based plastic,
no doubt) & I pump gas, breathe fumes,
listen to the Stones sing, *It's a gas,*
all the while I'm occupied with time
& distance & their obliteration

& with the woman last night sleeping
outside on a bench, shouting, "Hey, mister,
you got food?" her back to me, yet turned
eyes white in lamp light—how had she known? I walked
on like the rest. Even the cop—
the old fart with crossed arms—ignored her.
"Hey, mister," again that voice a cliff,
an edge, a jump. I carried a clam-
shell of leftover curry (Massaman
with potatoes & onions & peanuts
& tofu & just the right hotness).
It glowed white in the dark. I was al-
most past her (elbow propped, blanketed
feet). "Hey, mister. I'm hungry."

                              I turned.
"Do you like hot food?" Her face confused.
"You know, spicy food?" Like that mattered.
"My mother's got a red bird pecking
at her medical bills." (Gray hair, knit
cap, wrinkles like me. Her mother? Still
alive?) The curry warmed her palm.
I hoped she had a spoon.

223

Back at Love's

#8, boat-tailed grackle returns.
Another lands on shit-stained sprinkler
& I think why not eat lunch right here
with the boom of traffic, the thick fumes,
hunger's obliteration minutes away.

So I eat my PB & blackstrap.
Golden-eye screeches his ascending
screech, his feathers all shine & sine wave
iridescent as the spilled diesel
& the cellophane wrapper scratching
the chorded concrete like a guitar pick—
Jumpin' Jack Flash, it's a gas, gas, gas!

Mrs. Grackle with her brown head strides
'round the corner of the car—she too
golden-eyed & erect & I wonder
about that other gas, that other
cure for the homeless & unwanted.
What birds eyed those prisoners as they
entered Dachau, Belzec, and Auschwitz—
pigeons, maybe, or crows? How did they
navigate that dust-clotted sky?

And what birds will still be here to watch
the last drop of this gas? Grackles, maybe,
though they nest in saltmarshes soon gone
to flood. Or Eurasian collared doves
that bob & coo from guardrail, black neck-
laces on backward.

The grackles keep
beseeching, *Hey, mister, hey, mister.*
And like Mick, big lips kissing his mic,
I frown at the crumbs of a crust of bread—
why not share just a bite—that's what they
golden-eye, not me. So I break crust

& toss. Third try he dives & catches.
The others chase him to the Love's sign.

Why not embrace all that is ugly
& holy & here—the grackle's song
that isn't a song, a breadcrumb dropped,
the shiny ribbon of gasoline
that will get me closer to home.

But it's all right now, in fact, it's a

Spoonbill

I.
The spoon of the bill
acts like a filter,
a trap to catch small
creatures whose shells
give feathers color—
roseate, scorching pink,
orange on the tail—
shrimp resurrected
to shining brilliance
rising each morning
to stoke sullen air
with flames.

II.
Love of a feather—
pink & soft & long,
bristly blue & sharp—
killed millions of birds:
spoonbills & crossbills,
flamingos & auks
upholstering hats
for derbies, the dead,
demure debutants.

III.
Do birds know the way
to forgive like they
navigate the stars?
Can they long-legged
wade muddy waters
of love's hurts & needs?
Surely spoonbill so
bright knows love
& how to forgive.

ROBERT MORGAN has published several volumes of poetry, most recently *Terroir* (Penguin, 2011) and *Dark Energy* (Penguin, 2015). His novels include *Gap Creek*, 1999, *New York Times* bestseller, and *Chasing the North Star*, 2016. His collections of short fiction include *As Rain Turns to Snow*, 2017, and *In the Snowbird Mountains*, 2023. Among his nonfiction books are *Boone: A Biography*, 2007, a national bestseller, and *Lions of the West; Heroes and Villains of the Westward Expansion*, 2011. *Fallen Angel: The Life of Edgar Allan Poe* was published in 2023. He has received fellowships and awards from the Guggenheim and Rockefeller Foundations, The National Endowment for the Arts, and an Academy Award from the American Academy of Arts and Letters. A native of Western North Carolina, he has taught since 1971 at Cornell University, where he is now Kappa Alpha Professor of English (Emeritus).

Acknowledgments

"Squirrel Hill"
    First published in *Cloudbank*
"Mandolin"
    First published in *Rattle*
"Cowbell"
    First published in *The Atlantic*
"Watching Clouds"
    First published in *Appalachian Places*

Squirrel Hill

In every summer storm it seemed,
in each electrical display,
a claw of fire would rake a tree
and blast to splinters trunk and limbs,
and whip roots out of steaming ground.
The explanation was that iron
deposits in the hill drew down
the lash of heaven's wrath, or some
magnetic river underground
reached up to claim the giant gift
of fire, as if the hill had veins
receptive to the awful power
of stormy revelation. Yet
on ordinary days the woods
on that acclivity were drab
and cluttered with the sad debris
of tempest rage and ecstasy.

Mandolin

When Grandma Cecil tickled her
bright mandolin below her chin
it seemed she scratched an itch
and shivered something near her heart.
With instrument in arms she was
oblivious to all of us
unsympathetic in-law kin.
Her playing was her best defense
in that awkward second marriage.
The mandolin was strange to us,
too short for an adult we thought,
its belly bulging like a goiter,
exotic with its teasing trills,
the pick a special fingernail
for etching deeper in the tune
a figure of excited loss,
her plucking an odd intimacy
with corridors and hidden rooms
that only she could see and would
conceal from her new family
with needling sting of melody.

Cowbell

We come across a ridge and hear
a cowbell in the cove beyond,
a tinkle sweetening the air
with vague rubato as the breeze
erases tones and then the notes
resume like echoes from the past
or from a cave inside the cliff,
a still, calm voice in dialect
and keeping its own company,
both out of time and long as time,
both here and from a higher sphere,
as if the voice of history
were intimate as memory.

Jehuda

When they asked me to lead them through
the dark and point out the master
they pretended they just meant
to question him about his work,
assess his doctrine in relation to
the Law. No one suggested torture,
nor any punishment, just talk,
and, certainly, no crucifixion.
I was misled from the first, set up,
with a promise to honor me
Passover night. How would you like
to be the one with no respect or
recognition from the rest?
Because I was short, I got no
consideration, was teased, my manhood
questioned by older married men
with families, who'd deserted homes
to follow him. And Kephas was
the worst: he spoke with that accent
from Galilee, but was heard, a mere
fisherman. That little squirt Johanan
got the most attention, just a boy
they favored every day, indulged
with honeycomb, allowed to sleep
beside the master on the coldest nights.
In walks along the dusty roads
I lagged behind to miss their jibes
and gather my own thoughts.
Sometimes I wondered why I stayed
with them, but something beyond
my understanding drew me on.
When rabbis of the synagogue
insisted that I guide them to
the leader I assented, as
they only sought to quiz our dear

instructor, learn about his new
beliefs, and judge the truth he preached.
There was no hint they would arrest
and whip my shepherd. How could I
imagine such a consequence?
And everybody has a right to earn
a coin for honest work. Now they
will not concede my innocence.
I meant no harm for the master,
and only served as pilot for
the elders, as anybody might,
not knowing a mob would gather
that awful night in such a place.
I face no future but a bleak abyss,
Gehenna, without a friend who
will remember me with gladness.
I'm cursed for all eternity,
but also a celebrity.

Watching Clouds

The first and final luxury
we can afford is hope, and time
for viewing clouds, those luminous
evolving fleets and flocks, the towers
of blinding conflagrations, cities
without population, world
on elevated world of silent mist,
and otherworlds that float on time
beyond time, on distant peaks
as wide and far as we can see,
a spectacle for our delight,
and, yes, a barrier against
despair and flimsy vanities,
when we are left with nothing but
this show above, cool oxygen,
magnificent as thunder's hush.

karla k. morton has sixteen poetry collections. A National Heritage Wrangler Award winner, Indies National Book Award winner, Foreword Book Award winner, Spur Award winner, Betsy Colquitt Award winner and E2C Grant recipient, she is guest editor for TCU Press's *Selected Works of Walt McDonald*. She is published in journals such as *The Southern Review, Atlanta Review, American Life in Poetry, Alaska Quarterly Review, Southword Literary Journal, Boulevard, Lascaux Review, Comstock Review*, and *New Ohio Review*. Her book with 2005 Texas State Poet Laureate Alan Birkelbach *The National Parks: A Century of Grace* (TCU Press) is historic, as it is the first book of poetry ever written in-situ from all sixty-two national parks. A percentage of royalties from the book goes back to the Parks System. Morton is the 2010 Texas State Poet Laureate and nominee for the National Cowgirl Hall of Fame.

Acknowledgments

"Tom Clark"
> First appeared in *Politics of the Minotaur* (Texas Review Press, 2021)

Secrets of the Gumbo

To you—the daughter, the son—
I give the Gumbo,
the meatloaf,
lemon squares with powdered sugar.

My wedding day, mother's perfect gift:
an album of all those recipes
murmured mother to child
behind wooden spoons
finally written down.

To you my daughter, my son—
I give the secrets of Gumbo:
that African word for okra;
so many ways to thicken
the bones, the brain,
the hidden heart.

In concentration camps, women gathered
"to smoke":
secretly spreading each cigarette paper—
sparing precious pencil lead
to record tiny recipes for children
they would never touch again;
threading them into the hems of their dresses
hoping *still* to pass them on.

To you, my daughters, my sons—
remember the pan-fried grilled cheese,
the tacos with corn,
the dark roux of chicken and andouille,

the way the house smelled
as you cantered in—
declaring the Gumbo pot so big,
it could feed the whole world.

Battlefield Cornbread

—a Civil War love letter

My Beloved,
Before this horrid war,
there was not one night we were *ever* apart.

I was thinking today
how there are no babies in the hunt.
How I've always stayed home
with the children
to keep the old stove stoked—
ready to cook what you just killed.

You now, starving on the battlefield—
with no knowledge of how to prepare
the grouse you just shot.

And I, starving at home—
with no knowledge
of how to catch a grouse.

Nothing can completely fortify
man and woman for war;
for survival without each other.

But here, Love,
a recipe for those lean nights:

Mix the cornmeal from your haversack
with a little pork fat
to make a stiff batter.
Spin your bayonet in it
until coated on both sides.
Hold it over the fire to cook the bread.

This, the one thing we can both do—
a moment we can think of each other

at the same time
as we lift it to our lips;

the sun quickly drifting dark,
the years between us, hungry and slow.

—Inspired by Theresa Crouse's "9 Civil War Recipes"

laissez les bon temps rouler

The shrill of spring flowers'
purple perfume, leggy vines,
the uncontainable pulse, thrum—

as if I were Persephone
stepping off the plane,
finally back in the country of *Sun*,

spreading arms to the bounty—
all jazz band and milk punch,
sugar cubes in champagne

all the while Hades fuming below,
standing on the furniture,
yanking down asphodels
one by one

peeping up;
his fat twitching iris
filling each dirty hole

Tom Clark

I am 98% certain that you, Tom Clark,
poet of *"Nux,"*
are not the same Tom Clark
I went to high school with—

a rodeo man, three years older,
who, as a senior, had already broken
most every bone in his body.

My crush was *huge*,
and he smelled so good
and dated Nancy Gidley.

But tonight, I'll let my mind
go down that path
and picture you as *my* Tom Clark,
actually knowing Latin,
a lover now of words;
grey sneaking into those
sandy curled tips of hair
at your shoulders;

your hand, stiff from writing—
your fingers, never quite the same
after that last ride in '82,
bucked off before eight seconds,
your palm crushed
by that old Brahma named Hank,
the one with the busted right horn.

Portent

Tucked up in the branches,
warbling of weather and luck,
of firm worms and warm ferns
and troves of mollusks,

thrushes sang its Latin origin:
Sign, taken.

I had a premonition deep in the Appalachians
that I would die from being crushed.
An oddly comforting portent.

No need to worry now—
just to live like jubilant birds
and Fibonacci-housed snails.

Who among us could be so charmed
to sing till dusk,
or perhaps, one day in late May,
to look back
and behold
a long, glistening trail
left behind.

RICK MULKEY is the author of *All These Hungers, Ravenous: New & Selected Poems, Toward Any Darkness, Bluefield Breakdown;* and *Before the Age of Reason.* With Denise Duhamel, he has edited the anthology *Ice on a Hot Stove: A Decade of Converse MFA Poetry.* Previous work has appeared in *The Georgia Review, Poet Lore, Shenandoah, Swamp Pink, The Literary Review, Poetry East, South Carolina Review,* and *Still: The Journal.* He currently teaches in the Low Residency MFA and directs the BFA in Creative Writing at Converse University. He lives in Spartanburg, South Carolina.

Acknowledgments

"Discovering an Abandoned Orchard Near Bluefield, VA"
     First appeared in *Still: The Journal*
"What My Mother Taught Me About Narrative"
     First appeared in *Swamp Pink*
"Late Summer Meditation on Van Gogh's Wheatfield with a Reaper'"
     First appeared in *MacQueen's Quinterly*

Discovering an Abandoned Orchard Near Bluefield, VA

Some think it's in our best interest
to prune fruit trees of watersprouts and sideshoots,
thinning the canopy to let in light and increase
the apple crop, but I believe the right course

is to follow the northern wind to its own conclusion
down a worn deer run where like an old white-tail buck
we stop to savor what ripens before the frost
consumes it all. And be thankful for the time

we had to wander the abandoned orchard,
bed down in the shade-cooled grass, relaxed
and unfettered from any human task
the world, fortunately, never imagined for us.

Second Spring

She walks to her garden to water plants
well past their prime, most now turning to seed,
the living blooms pale compared to summer's
early gaudiness. Still she knows a quick soak
won't hurt, and she hates to see the season end.

Garden hose in her right hand and cultivator hoe
to clear weeds that fair well no matter
how dry September has been, in her left hand,
she goes about her chore: bending, pulling, watering.
Then a pause as she turns the nozzle off
and sets her hoe aside. She's on her knees digging

with both hands when she looks back toward me
and smiles. "Blooms," she calls. "I thought they died,
but here they are." She points to a clump
of small, bright petals hidden beneath zinnia
that thrived all summer, and now are thinning out
to let sunlight through where there'd been only shade.

Days from first frost, the dianthus have arrived.
Such a small thing to offer her joy.
A reminder that even in a long life
a little light can bring the unexpected,
a moment we hadn't even known to miss:

a wife barefoot in grass, a garden hose in hand,
and a smile on that mouth I'd forgotten
to kiss when earlier I woke beside her.

What My Mother Taught Me About Narrative

I'm watching her disappear in a Tampa hospital room,
her breath rasping, her lips swollen and cracked,
my father standing outside the door, his hands stuffed
inside his pockets to stop their shaking. It's an image
I'll want to discard, but the consequence of age
is memory: both its presence and its absence,
its truth and lies. It's the inevitable byproduct of life,
stories we didn't mean to write, but the pen
scratched out each letter's line and curve anyway.

I'm sure my mother, all of seventeen when she discovered
she was pregnant, had imagined she'd author
a different tale than this one scripted from her bone and flesh,
her eyes, her pain and pleasure. She hadn't planned
to bear an allegory for how her life could be,
but there I was. Here I am, a narrative twist,
a new vocabulary, my birth photo beside the definition
for surprise. And how surprised years later
when she reached to touch her breast and found it there,
that fibrous knot, that kernel sentence for an ending
which would write itself. We all want some stories

to last a little longer. The evening before she died,
I sat with her and promised I'd always remember
what a beautiful mother she had been,
but, of course, none of us can make that guarantee.
My wife, who fears her mother's dementia may one day
be her own, writes down everything she sees and hears
in case one night it disappears. So, when I consider
that moment in the hospital, I worry the final line
I told my mother was a fiction. That's why there are
certain words and phrases I'll never say again.

I've grown tired of how like an old Faber eraser
life strips the surface away leaving only the illusion

of new and clean. And now I only believe in plot
when music is absent. I only believe in memory
where there's nothing left to imagine. For instance,
what if I tell you I never made my mother that promise?
Perhaps it's just a story I tell myself
to make her ending seem a little kinder.

Late Summer Meditation on Van Gogh's
Wheatfield with a Reaper

Summer's fevered gauze drapes heavily over the garden,
tree limbs turn slack and wilt in August's sun.
The clay earth cracks open beneath the blades
of yellowing grass. Even songbirds grow quiet
soon after sunrise, then hide away the day
wherever shade allows it. Still the sky lures
me out from the house into the shimmering silence.
There is no talking, and the wind begins to cast off
the worries I spent the morning scratching over,
blind mole tunneling for the sake of digging.
Sure, there's danger in the world. Only surface tension
keeps the walls from falling in. Everything will die.
But let it be in sunlight, so when we see it coming,
the reaper's blade will be bright and shining.

Fathers and Sons

What do we know of our fathers, really?
Except eventually we become them
and understand even less of ourselves.
Each spring my father plowed his single acre,
too little land to matter, too much for one man
to till alone from end to end. I followed
collecting rocks and roots the earth had swallowed,
clearing out the tillage rows to plant
fresh seeds, wait for green sprouts
along straight rows where the hillside's wavering
curve once lay. He crisscrossed open ground
leaving welts along the earth the way years earlier
his father's maple rod snapped across his thighs
to teach a boy respect, to be his best,
a lesson taught so well, that as a man,
my father pushed beyond his will to quit
or rest in the shade of apple boughs.
Beneath his bent back and steady gate,
the tiller's blades sliced into soil.
Black loam turned over, opening itself
to him like the spine of a book.
I traced his steps, lines across a page,
imagining when I'd become a man myself.

JIM MURPHY is the author of four poetry collections: *The Memphis Sun* (Kent State UP), *Heaven Overland* (Kennesaw State UP), *The Uniform House* (Negative Capability Press) and *Versions of May* (Negative Capability Press). His poems have appeared in or are forthcoming from *Brooklyn Review*, *Cimarron Review*, *Gulf Coast*, *Painted Bride Quarterly*, *Mississippi Review*, *Puerto del Sol*, *Texas Review*, *The Southern Review*, *TriQuarterly* and other journals. He has also translated a chapbook of poems from Spanish, *Amazonia*, by Colombian-American poet Juan Carlos Galeano. He lives in Birmingham, Alabama, and is Professor of English at the University of Montevallo.

A History of Red Mountain

Was there always the premonition of a city here?
Were there always hints in the striations, deflections,
water cool in the Jones Valley bottom, down to the final
low rumble of the Appalachians and to the coastal plains,
at last rolling slowly into the salt jaws of the open Gulf?

No. There was a time when there was only untelling rock,
before that just a burning mass—the very thing that was
ceded into molten steel. *Yes.* It has been here so long
that the Heaviest Corner on Earth, the high quartet that
quietly looms at 20th Street and 1st Avenue downtown
was present all along, only hidden in the landscape.

So there are mysteries among these veins of hematite,
rusted rock faces, and jagged sockets gouged from hard,
unceasing work. All these textures must mean something
that adds up to a social system, a business-minded dream
where progress is a golden spiral upwards, a lucid beam
that flattens lifetimes into papers, into pixels, into a road
that cuts along the ragged mountain, and then turns away.

All the mines are finished here, their darkness undisturbed.
Above, a decayed reminder—*This Red Mountain Iron Ore
is Basis of Birmingham's Iron-Steel Industry*—stamped
in white metal now corroded, partly blasted, partly gone.
Drivers wind the center of some questions underneath—
*How long until I'm there? Did I pass or fail? What is it
worth to me?*—and other variations, making up our days.

When the bend is silent, when the crumpled guardrail
is taken out, and the plastic sputter has been cleaned,
what resonates but the rock itself, its voiceless lecture
on what's hidden and what's seen? We peopled this
place with a kind of pain that could break diamonds.
One way or another, we hammer its traces to history.

Full Arkestra

Knowledge is laughable when attributed to a human being.
—Sun Ra

And so in Birmingham, bleeder of talent,
bereft of the jazz magic landed in this place,
the bright Saturnine homeland you don't have
to go far to find is now enshrined in the record
store, cool as the moon, and just as bright.

> *When a piano falls in outer space*
> *does it make a sound?*

Visitors come in all sizes, all hours of the night.
If you listen close, you can see their hands
aflame, as they gesture toward your mind,
your heart, your hands that always move to
somehow key that silver music of the spheres.

> *He's not crazy, you know.*
> *He's just got a mind out of time.*

There's nothing ancient about this unquiet
Egypt. When you own it, when you are worn,
monumentally enrobed and vested in it, only
then do the chords leap forward. You don't need
to drop dynasties when that stylus hits the groove.

> *Heads bob. Outside the flood.*
> *Is this hell or Arkadelphia?*

It must be a thing about the so-called end of days
that casts worry on the people. You get only
so far into any prophecy before it comes out
in questions, in a chromatic blaze of saxophones,
in the open smiles of children who know better.

No matter how they try to hide it,
space is the place it all goes down.

When you think about it, there's no such thing
as silence. There's no distant, cantilevered place
that the Beautiful can't reach if you compress
it into measures, send it off in blue notes of hope
all the way out there. And so in Birmingham.

This Way to Creosote Falls

Timberland—more than two thirds of Alabama
by pure acreage, ninety-four percent of that
in private hands—but such cash registers almost
nothing here, in the inner suburbs that ring this
struggling city.

                Take a child from school.
Place that child in the midst of a pine plantation
before sundown on the hottest day of August,
when the cicadas drone over stillness, and the air
is like the inside of a wood wardrobe, and what
will happen next is less than magic—the supposition
that this place is wilderness, that wolves and bobcats
rove the perfect rows, and the threats that snake
behind those shinbone trunks are real, and manifold.

Remove yourself from history and all the wood
of memory heaves from the ground, then goes
straight into the mill-jaws, debarked and band-sawed
as its dust of recollection swirls.

                         My great
grandfather knocked around during the Depression,
went broke, then signed on to a turpentine camp.
Worked himself sick carving cat faces into trees,
getting at the resin. He left with nothing
but wore down bones and never was the same.

These are words from another world. They are
repeated to remind the kids their lives are easy,
beer in hand on a summer day, watching meat
sizzle on the shiny deck.

                  There's a lot of story
but no lore in getting rich.

Take your mother's grandfather—a railroad man.
Started out underage as a regular gandy dancer,
a section hand who tamped and drove and lined
the tracks and worked that way for cheap.
After the war, he was put up by the government
in a Quonset hut on the University quad.
Got his Bachelor's of Forestry and then worked
the rest of his life under an air conditioner.
Remember that next time that you skip class.

And what to tell the child today?

                    If you want
to spend next year as a Fellow in New York,
you'd better get at least a 3.6 at Sewanee.
Do you think that it's all free?

                    The ties went on forever,

so they said, and then they stopped. The process
was halted suddenly between tar and creosote.
The preservative was cancerous. The pilings
lurched sideways in the water. And no one said
a blessed word.

                    Tomorrow at noon, not even
in the same country as those faded paper ancestors,
read over the broken warnings and instructions
in six languages for your children's new treehouse.
Read carefully because as a parent, that's your job.
And even as you crouch beside the greening fence,
as the Ray-Bans slip down your nose from sweat,
you'll find no trace of what it means to be cut down.

BRADY PETERSON lives near Belton, Texas, where for twenty-nine years he worked building houses and teaching rhetoric. He is the author of *Glued to the Earth, Between Stations, Dust, From an Upstairs Window, García Lorca Is Somewhere in Produce*, and *At the Edge of Town*.

Acknowledgments

"Fault Lines"
        First published in *García Lorca Is Somewhere in Produce*
"Chant" and "I Shall Pick the Flowers Myself"
        First published in *From an Upstairs Window*
"The Sound of Retreat" and "The Ferry"
        First published in *At the Edge of Town*

Fault Lines

I live on the edge of black gumbo farm land
to the east and fractured limestone mesas
that defined west for me. From the dam,
I see both vistas. One stretches toward the gulf
with red snapper, shrimp, and words like bayou.
The other seems like another planet—I expect
to see a different sun, maybe a second moon.

Before the dam, on a back road now under
the deep blue green waters of a lake, I kissed
a girl one sparkling afternoon after bathing
in the river. We lay in the grass and laughed.
How simple and easy—the music on the car radio
as we drove back to town. It must have been
Saturday.

Kennedy and Diem were months dead—the FBI
fumbling to decipher The Kingsmen—*every night at ten*—
what were the words—*all kinds of ways . . .*
We stop for hamburgers and fries. We lie to each
other, knowing but somehow still believing
the possibility of a different world, of an extra moon.
The god damn moon.

I look east and south and wonder how long
it would take to float the river to its mouth.

Chant

Soffit is a builder's word, a carpenter's word—
like fascia and header and stud. Top plate
and joist. Soffit though has a mantra quality.
Whisper it over and over as you slip into deep
meditation: *soffit, soffit, soffit* . . .

As if to quietly call the angels to your side,
whispering low so they have to move in close
to hear. What is it you want, they ask—*nothing*.
What is it you want—*nothing*.
Want being deceiver's word, a labyrinth.

The soffit seals the attic, keeping out squirrels
and raccoons, though a determined creature
may find its way in. You set out a trap.
Raccoon may be a mantra word as well,
though you hesitate to use it.

It's raining. You check for leaks,
an old habit. You listen to the rain
as if the patterns were code one deciphers,
rain being a sacred gift—like air.
What is it you want—*nothing*.

You are dry and warm inside your house.
Puddles form on the driveway.

I Shall Pick the Flowers Myself

September, and I am already pushing spring
in my mind, though winter is pleasant enough—
no mosquitos. Late August showers, spindly rain
lilies—don't remember seeing them before—
showing themselves for a few days.

I saw you working your garden, bent over a row
of beans—driving by last week, last month
it may have been—wishing I could paint
the impression, but am more than a hundred
years too late.

Too late to celebrate the feelings one once had,
Virginia says, before the light of shell fire
revealed the world—puffed and stuffed
with straw—still I saw you working your garden,
wanted to paint you there—

Mixing colors on a palette, white cotton trousers—
as in wearing them cuffed—greens and browns,
wildflowers on the side of the road, lazy susans
and daisies—brushed yellows. Summer gives
way to September—then October.

Pumpkins and cranberries, whipped cream
and whiskey in your coffee, a twinge of regret—

The Sound of Retreat

This is what it is like when you lose a country.
He sips his coffee and looks out the window
at the dreary rain. It has rained for forty days,
it seems. He looks for animals pairing.

It's only the rain.
A gray cloudy drizzle, making it impossible
for the plumber to dig up the collapsed
pipe going from his washer to the septic tank.

It will be $750 dollars, the plumber
tells him. Good thing, I'm rich, he mutters.
It's a line he uses at the check out
when buying groceries.

He reads a commentary about the President,
about the takeover of justice—just another brick . . .
Down the street a neighbor flies the flag
in front of his house—even in the rain.

He remembers learning flag decorum
as a boy, growing up on post, how they stood
attention for retreat every afternoon at five.
How he believed that if he let the flag drag the ground—

just touch the ground.

But that was a time when history mattered—
even if diluted.
No mention of Sand Creek or the Philippines.
Nothing about exemptions for Texas
when Mexico abolished slavery in 1829.

But history mattered, he says as he bends
over to tie his shoe.

The Ferry

We each drink a warm beer and talk
the world into being.
Tanks roll into the city, we scurry
across the rooftop,
wait for choppers to fly us
to an offshore carrier, wait to go home,
though I fear home has been misplaced.

I ride the bus to Dallas.
You head for Seattle, where you intend
to ride the ferry there back and forth
to and from Bainbridge Island.
I walk to Dealey Plaza
and sit on the grass.

At night sometimes, I speak to you
as if we were still young,
as if angels had wings.

CATHERINE PIERCE is the Poet Laureate of Mississippi and the author of four books of poems: *Danger Days* (2020), *The Tornado Is the World* (2016), *The Girls of Peculiar* (2012), and *Famous Last Words* (2008), all from Saturnalia Books. Her work has appeared in *The Best American Poetry*, the *New York Times*, *American Poetry Review*, *The Nation*, *The Southern Review*, the Academy of American Poets Poem-a-Day series, and elsewhere. A recipient of fellowships from the National Endowment for the Arts and the Academy of American Poets, and a two-time Pushcart Prize winner, Pierce teaches at Mississippi State University.

Acknowledgments

"If/When"
    First published in *The Southern Review*
"The Dog Greets the Tornado"
    First published in *The Tornado Is the World* (Saturnalia, 2016)
"Chadwick Lake, 8:15 a.m."
    First published in *Danger Days* (Saturnalia, 2020)

If/When

The poem I planned to write
was about last week's hurricane,

about how I live in Mississippi,
not so far from the storm's rages,

and how even still we felt
nothing here, nothing at all.

That was going to be the ending,
because I wanted to make a point

about how easy it is to ignore
disaster when it's not churning

directly over your town, and I was hoping
a reader might then extrapolate

a larger point about disturbance
and proximity, like how politicians

are always saying they used to oppose X
until some terrible Y happened

to their daughters, and it seems
to me we're requiring an awful lot

from daughters these days. Sons, too.
This week a message from my kids'

school district included the phrase *if/when
a lockdown is ever necessary.* The reason

I'm writing this poem instead
of the one I'd planned is that I keep

thinking about that email and also
now the hurricane was a week ago

and there's a new disturbance
forming near the Bahamas. And

last night Sioux Falls was tornado-
shredded and in Sterling, Colorado,

egg-size hail pummeled windshields,
and I guess what I'm saying is, why bother

with a poem about one hurricane,
one email? There will be more,

and there will be more,
and there will be more until

there is nothing left. The thing
about the poem I was going to write

is that it would have been a lie.
That nonsense about how we don't

feel it here. We feel it everywhere,
don't we? Dear daughter, dear son,

dear someone's something, we're well
past the *if* and into the *when*.

Talk about proximity—
some days I wear the world

like a skin. I am tired of waiting
for extrapolation. Let us all

be disturbances now.

The Dog Greets the Tornado

Hello one-not-like-me. Hello
to your great tail. You are larger
than the truck that takes me
to the woods and back. You are larger
than the house I sometimes go in.
I see you coming close. I am blown
back on myself. My teeth buzz.

Today I caught a squirrel. Today
I dug a patch of earth bare and slept
for a while. It was a good day.

You are so large. The man is inside
the house. I feel my haunches needling up.

And now the brown trees are below me.
The house is below me. The man
is below me. I am part of the sky.
I hear you howling. You must
have learned that from me.

Chadwick Lake, 8:15 a.m.

You're trying to make the lake
something it isn't. You're trying
to make it a mirror, a meditation,
a mother. You're trying, at least,
to make it a lake, but it isn't even that.
It's a half-lake, at best. It's half-filled
with cattails and sludge. There's a white bag
caught in the weeds. A bright yellow
bulldozer where there should be glint
and mallards. Why can't you be
satisfied with the not-quite lake?
What are you still hoping might
surprise you? Why do you persist
in looking for a crisp mountain sky
when you know you live half
a country from the mountains?
Why are you always waiting for that day
in late October when the leaves
and the air and the distant hay smell
are all in exact and perfect proportion
to one another? Don't you know
that's a sure way to go through life
as if you've swallowed a tiny burning marble?
Look at these tread marks in the mud,
aren't they their own small arrows of beauty?
Look at those cattails, don't they bend like
any meadow flower or Adirondack fern?
So what if the ducks have flown off?
So what if the turtles have vanished?
Can't you love the black plastic construction
fence, the diggers, the plumes of exhaust?
The white bag keeps blowing, though
there's no wind today. You walk closer.
It's an egret. Its long neck curved to preen,
feathers bright as the camera's flash
at the moment everyone says *surprise*.

LYNN POWELL has published three books of poetry—*Old & New Testaments*, *The Zones of Paradise*, and *Season of the Second Thought* —and a book of nonfiction, *Framing Innocence*. Her honors include a National Endowment for the Arts Fellowship, the Felix Pollak Prize in Poetry, the Brittingham Prize in Poetry, the Studs & Ida Terkel Award for Nonfiction, and four Ohio Arts Council Excellence Awards. Born and raised in East Tennessee, she has lived in Oberlin, Ohio, since 1990. After a variety of other teaching and professional adventures, she taught poetry, nonfiction, and pedagogy for sixteen years in the Creative Writing Program of Oberlin College, where she founded and directed the Writers in the Schools Program.

Acknowledgments

"No Proust, No Stevens, No Nietzsche" and "Aubade for the Muse"
    From *Season of the Second Thought* by Lynn Powell.
    Reprinted by permission of the University of Wisconsin Press.
    © 2017 by the Board of Regents of the University of Wisconsin
    System. All rights reserved.

Unsent Lines
for R.B.

High up in my heart's hierarchy of kisses
is the one you gave me—that slow, eloquent question
of a kiss one autumn afternoon on a Tennessee hilltop.
We must have climbed up there to talk
in the tongue-tied finesse of the young.
Whatever else we said that day that kiss undid,
confirmed, denied, and fixed us at a brink.

I had a dream of you that winter—angel in a spangled
loincloth, glitter in your long black hair,
your head thrown back and all the chaste, raucous, gap-toothed
joy of the cosmos rumbling out of you as laughter, shaking
your fine, unapologetic mountain belly.

Five hundred miles—a ballad's worth of miles—away,
I read now of the life you made, and of the art
you taught yourself, stroke by bright stroke,
self-named *fauve* of the Appalachian foothills.
You said a hundred portraits would be your apprenticeship,
but you couldn't stop looking into face
after face in your ravaged coalfield town.
You sketched each face on a grid then lifted into life
the eccentric dignity of the molasses maker,
the fireman with flames leaping in his visor,
the cornered child orphaned by opioids, the hunter
who obliged and aimed his rifle at you.

In the middle—as it turns out—of your life,
you sent me poems, and I sent you mine.
I remember a "silver-throated creek" in a line
so right I wanted to keep it in lines of my own.

Every elegy is too late. But some are selfish, too,
craving bright shards of our young selves lodged in other minds
and grieving when they go dark.

Poem Beginning with Lines by Lynn Powell, Age 22

South, I had no suppleness of thought.
I acquiesced to the hot azalea—

and to Lord knows what else both
south and north of the Mason-Dixon line.

Acquiesced? I agree
with those succulent syllables

but not with their scent of surrender.
Chose would be more like it, even if

I did outsource my will to pheromones
and a Biblical need to *know.*

Late fall in the Finger Lakes, 500 miles
from anything resembling a bloom

except goldenrod gone viral—
and a girl hiking into another gaudy sunset

with another inscrutable boy.
15,000 days since then and what's left?

A yellowed page of shy striptease?
Typed study of herself in black and white

and pink? But who am I
to judge? I who sought and, somehow,

found my life
through her hothouse ways.

No Proust, No Stevens, No Nietzsche

I.
What got thought elsewhere, stayed elsewhere—
except for mail sent to our Chattanooga mailbox,
galvanized at the end of a new dead end.

I watched for the mailman's car from the perch
of my Schwinn Starlet, or from the porch if *the devil
was beating his wife* (the sun bright in spite

of an outburst of rain). On good days: the "family
bulletin" from Uncle Duck—cigar-haunted onionskin
with smudged news of Harlan and Georgia,

floozy jokes, and gibes at screwloose yankees.
And on best days: the only novels I knew to read,
fresh from the refiner's fire of *Reader's Digest*.

II.
We got close enough to kiss, but then
that boy stood up and forced a different laying on
of hands, for he knew God was everywhere

and especially in East Tennessee.
Repent! and he *meant* it, looking down on me
with the seasoned glare of an exorcist.

I glared back but let him do
what he was going to do to my harlot soul.
In his grandma's knick-knacked

living room, there were no swine, though,
no serpents, not even hot coals in the Franklin stove—
no place for that demon to go but further in.

III.
Barbeque and Jack Daniels for the famous poet,
which I suppose they thought was clever that far north
of the Mason-Dixon Line.

And I was introduced, fresh from the hills,
as poetic kin. *I know what I'd like to do with that
young thang*, he winked to his peers.

I hated how prettily I flushed, how my words
froze, but I was Southern, startled, and young enough
to laugh it off. In time I learned to chalk him up

to another weak man in exile—though not
so far gone as a girl in the small boat of her thought,
adrift in the gale force of language.

Aubade for the Muse

A flutter at the threshold—
and here you are, nothing between us

but a throw rug and a hothouse lily.
Rosy and rugged, you grin

like a man who's spent a thousand nights
with a thousand soft-skinned books.

Last time you breezed in,
you had more critiques than a prophet

workshopping the Israelites.
You said I needed more *original* sins.

You nixed my metaphor and left
my ode blundering into bloom

against the glistening odds of the frost.
Who let you back inside my dream?

Toned down in khakis and crewneck,
you settle on the couch and trot out

that old line about needing me
to "flesh out" your "big idea."

Who knows? Maybe soon—maybe even before
the alarm—you'll recant the rant

and the razzmatazz and give me what
you know I always want: your speechless

mouth on mine, making it all up.

OCTAVIO QUINTANILLA is the author of the poetry collection, *If I Go Missing*, the founder and director of the literature & arts festival, VersoFrontera, publisher of Alabrava Press, and former Poet Laureate of San Antonio, TX. His Frontextos (visual poems) have been published and exhibited widely. His new poetry collection, *The Book of Wounded Sparrows*, is forthcoming from Texas Review Press in fall 2024. He teaches literature and creative writing at Our Lady of the Lake University. Website: octavioquintanilla.com.

Where Do We Go from Here?

Once, I felt I didn't fit into my own name. Felt too big for me, like an oversized shirt. When you cross a river from the south to call the land in the north your new Motherland, your name follows you like an injured dog, and also your history. My father is buried in South Texas, close to the river he crossed undocumented countless times to work, to live, to love. He's the first of kin to permanently find a home in this country. With a first-grade education from Mexico, this man built an empire of possibilities. Now the children of his children speak Spanish all mocho, Tex-Mex, Frontera-speak, and they have no accents, and they graduate college, and they find their future here and not elsewhere, like those who came before them did. Our dead are here now. Their descendants keep growing like trees. Does this mean that we have finally earned the right to truly say, "We belong here"? In this country? In this land? In this moment?

The Poetics of Separation: A Micro-Essay

Poetry remembers that distance can be made of suffering.

Distance between blood cells.

Between two words on this page.

Between a mother and a son.

And so, I carry my past like a bag full of dirt,
but I can't make words grow out of it
and write what I can't remember:

What is the Spanish word for *water*?
What is the Spanish word for *longing*?
What is the Spanish word for *failure*?

My relationship with language is absence,
one I can't shape with my hands.

Not like clay.
Or fire.

I try.

And for this trying, I rely on what my body thinks it knows.

I allow it to speak to that part of me for which I'll never have words.

This poem doesn't want to tell you a story that you can follow.

It wants to take you to a river, blindfold you,

lower you into its veins.

Self-Portrait with My Father's Eyes

What sum of those who've died still remains with us? What percentage of our memory still belongs to them? When we see our shadow rising against a wall as we walk down a street, does it belong to us? Or is it the way a loved one who has died attempts to say, *I am here.*

Once, I painted a portrait of my father, face made of lines, and within the lines, I could see what I thought had always belonged to me: his eyes, and the way they looked at me, the way he looked at me, like a stranger looks at someone he loves.

Desaparecer

It's a scientific fact that if you keep your eyes
open for a long period of time,
eventually, all that you see, will disappear.
Like the word *disappear* disappears
in its Spanish translation: *desaparecer*.

Can you hear the traces of what's left,
of what's carried over?

What is left is the chameleon who can move
its eyes in two directions at once,
and not once will you move twice
to save your life.

Desaparecer: meaning *don't get lost, don't die,*
come home,

and your home, empty of metaphors,
and your metaphors, empty of mercy,

and you find yourself either writing
about a quiet country
that you no longer remember,

or about a name that still hurts you
when you dare whisper it in the dark rooms
of your empty kingdom.

Maybe we should be friends: I'll be
your accomplice, the *I* pronouncing itself,
the eye that stays open so you can see
the truth in the opposite of *disappear*.

Don't worry about this now,
for even if you lose your sense of sight,

you'll still be able to see your dreams.
You'll be able to see what they who burn
without light can't.

How do you quantify the fractions
of your life that have nothing to do
with seeing?

Tell me and I will tell you
that sometimes I wake trembling
at not finding you next to me,
and I fall asleep feeling the opposite
of holy, untranslated

on the blank of your face,
and I see nothing left
to carry me over.

Poem About Not Dying
(with references to the movie *Blood In, Blood Out*)

It's hard to write a funny poem about a movie
where a young boy dies
with a needle in his arm,
in a city where "vatos locos forever"
means that "You are on the clock, bitch,
and midnight is coming,"
where it means that no one gets to truly raise a family
and all the family you have
could backstab when you least expect it,
or will die for you
because this is the only way
they can show their love.
But love is everywhere,
just like in every neighborhood,
in every barrio there must be a pine tree
waiting for us to return.
It doesn't have to be a pine tree,
any tree would do,
but one on which one of our working-class forefathers,
just before the horizon swelled
with twilight,
carved their initials with a pocket knife
right in its heart's center.
For months now, I watch the same movies
over and over till I memorize
the lines the dying speak
just before they close their eyes forever
in a make-believe world
that sometimes spills into my dreams,
dreams where I am driving fast and reckless
like El Gallo Negro,
and my immigrant father dying
in the backseat,
asking for a drink of water,

his last, he says,
before he closes his eyes to this earth
and opens them
to see a new world
where everyone is a stranger
and words are birds
whose flight no one
understands.
Next time you see birds
think of them as words
we never say to each other,
like *I miss you*,
and *I love you*,
and *don't go*.
See the sky speak with birds
all along the dirt roads
where we try to leave a trace of who we are,
and hear them speak along grain fields
that brighten against the long horizon
like low flames,
or like the small fire a gun spits out of its mouth
into the air
to remind us
that it's just a movie,
that no one dies here,
and we all go home.

RON RASH is the author of the PEN/Faulkner finalist and *New York Times* bestselling novel *Serena*, in addition to the critically acclaimed novels *The Risen, Above the Waterfall, The Cove, One Foot in Eden, Saints at the River*, and *The World Made Straight*; five collections of poems; and seven collections of stories, among them *Burning Bright*, which won the 2010 Frank O'Connor International Short Story Award, *Nothing Gold Can Stay*, a *New York Times* bestseller, and *Chemistry and Other Stories*, which was a finalist for the 2007 PEN/Faulkner Award. His work has been translated into eighteen languages. Three times the recipient of the O. Henry Prize, he teaches at Western Carolina University. His latest novel, *The Caretaker*, was published by Knopf Doubleday in 2023.

Acknowledgments

"Black-eyed Susans," "Wolf Laurel," and "Speckled Trout"
    First published in *Raising the Dead*
"July 1949"
    First published in *Eureka Mill*
"Good Friday, 1995, Driving Westward"
    First published in *Among the Believers*

Black-Eyed Susans

The hay was belt-buckle high
when rain let up, three-days' sun
baked stalks dry, and by midday
all but the far pasture mowed,
raked into wind rows, above
June sky still blue so I drove
my tractor up on the ridge
to the far pasture where strands
of sagging barbed wire marked where
my land stopped, church land began,
knowing I'd find some grave-gift,
flowers, flag, Styrofoam cross
blown on my land, and so first
walked the boundary, made sure what
belonged to the other side
got returned, soon enough saw,
black-eyed susans, the same kind
growing in my yard, tied to
the bow a tight-folded note.
Always was all that it said,
which said enough for I knew
what grave that note belonged to,
and knew as well who wrote it,
she and him married three months
when he died, now always young,
always their love in first bloom,
too new to life to know life
was no honeymoon. Instead,
she learned that lesson with me
over three decades, what fires
our flesh set early on cooled
by time and just surviving,
and learned why old folks called it
getting hitched, because like mules
so much of life was one long row

you never saw the end of,
and always he was close by,
under a stone you could see
from the porch, wedding picture
she kept hid in her drawer,
his black-and-white flash-bulb grin
grinning at me like he knew
he'd made me more of a ghost
to her than he'd ever be.
There at that moment—that word
in my hand, his grave so close,
if I'd had a shovel near
I'd have dug him up right then,
hung his bones up on the fence
like a varmint, made her see
what the real was, for memory
is always the easiest
thing to love, to keep alive
in the heart. After awhile
I lay the note and bouquet
where they belonged, never spoke
a word about it to her
then or ever, even when
she was dying, calling his
name with her last words. Sometimes
on a Sunday afternoon
I'll cross the pasture, make sure
her stone's not starting to lean,
if it's early summer bring
black-eyed susans for her grave,
leave a few on his as well,
for soon enough we'll all be
sleeping together, beyond
all things that ever mattered.

Carolina Parakeet

Though once plentiful enough
to pulse an acre field, green
a blue sky, they were soon gone,
whole flocks slaughtered in a day,
though before forever lost
found last here, in these mountains
so sparely settled a man
late as 1900 might
look up from new-broken land
and glimpse that bright vanishing.

Wolf Laurel

Tree branches ice-shackled, ground
hard as an anvil, three sons
and a father leave the blaze
huddled around all morning,
wade snow two miles where they cross
Wolf Laurel Creek, poke rifles
in rock holes, cliff leans hoping
to quarry what's killed five sheep,
but no den found as the ridge
sips away the gray last light
of winter solstice, and they
head back toward home, the trail
falling in blur-dark and then
the father falls too, eyes locked,
wrist unpulsed, the sons without
lantern, enough lingering light,
know they must leave him or risk
all of them lost, know what waits
for death in this place, so break
a hole in Wolf Laurel's ice,
come back at first light to find
the creek's scab of cold covered
with snowdrift, circling paw prints
brushed away that sons might see
a father's face staring through
the ice as through a mirror.

Speckled Trout

Water-flesh gleamed like mica:
orange fins, red flankspots, a char
shy as ginseng, found only
in spring-flow gaps, the thin clear
of faraway creeks no map
could name. My cousin showed me
those hidden places. I loved
how we found them, the way we
followed no trail, just stream-sound
tangled in rhododendron,
to where slow water opened
a hole to slip a line in,
and lift as from a well bright
shadows of another world,
held in my hand, their color
already starting to fade.

July 1949

This is what I cannot remember—
a young woman stooped in a field,
a hoe callousing her hands,
the rows stretching out like hours.
And this woman, my mother, rising
to dust rising half a mile
up the road, the car
she has waited days for
realized in the trembling heat.

It will rust until spring, the hoe
dropped at the field's edge.
She is running toward the car,
the sandlapper relatives who spill out
coughing mountain air with lint-filled lungs,
running toward the half-filled grip
she will learn to call a suitcase.

She is dreaming another life,
young enough to believe
it can only be better—
indoor plumbing, eight-hour shifts, a man
who cannot hear through the weave room's
roar the world's soft click,
fate's tumblers falling into place,
soft as the sound of my mother's
bare feet as she runs,
runs toward him, toward me.

Good Friday, 1995, Driving Westward

This day I feel I live among strangers.
The old blood ties beckon so I drive west
to Buncombe County, a weedy graveyard
where my rare last name crumbles on stone.

All were hardshell Baptists, farmers
who believed the soul is another seed
that endures when flesh and blood are shed,
that all things planted rise toward the sun.

I dream them shaking dirt off strange new forms.
Gathered for the last harvest, they hold hands,
take their first dazed steps toward heaven.

CHELSEA RATHBURN is the author of three poetry collections, most recently *Still Life with Mother and Knife* (LSU Press, 2019), winner of the 2020 Eric Hoffer Prize in Poetry. Born and raised in Florida, she has called Georgia home since 2001 and currently teaches at Mercer University in Macon. Since 2019, she has served as the Poet Laureate of Georgia.

Acknowledgments

"The Locksmith"
    First appeared in *Copper Nickel*
"On the Lam" and "Combustibles"
    First appeared in *Birmingham Poetry Review*

The Locksmith
—Miami, 1993

After the hurricane blew out our doors and windows
and we learned to live in the half-dark of boarded frames,
the man who arrived at last to fit the locks

on our new glass doors couldn't help tell us how
he'd just been inside Sylvester Stallone's new digs
and seen splendors we wouldn't believe, fountains

and moats, and scores of men working. *Go right,*
he said, *past Madonna's mansion* (he'd changed
the locks there too)—*look for the iron gate.*

And though I'd never seen *Rocky* or *Rambo,*
my family drove past the next weekend, the wonders
we hoped to see all locked behind a wall,

and I didn't mention that I'd been on that street before.
It ended at a waterfront park I knew
from another story: a classmate had gone there once

alone, probably skipping class, and a stranger
blocked the bayside path and took her arm.
She broke away but knew that if she ran,

she'd never reach her car, and so she jumped
off the seawall, not knowing how deep the water,
or if he'd follow and push her under. The man

stayed on the shore, and her feet found the bottom—
it must have been low tide—so she waded
toward the mansions, not yet bought up by singers

and movie stars, and the man, who must have sensed
a threat, a girl who might do anything,
trailed along a while, calling her crazy,

then loped away. She said she stayed in the water
a long time before climbing back to land.
I'd asked why she took judo after school.

We were standing by the lockers, and I knew—
something in her description of the man—
I knew I'd seen him too, in that same park

on a day I'd had the fortune not to be
alone. A brush with danger not unlike
a brush with fame. Years later I saw inside

Sly's house, in the pages of a magazine,
and I was struck not by the gardens and pools
that matched the locksmith's lavish descriptions,

but by the way the actor's face stared back
at him out of paintings and statues, making
the place a kind of monument to ego

as well as excess. They're forever linked in my mind,
the laborer, the actor, and the girl:
same street, same swath of shore, the difference

that power makes, the distance between the kinds
of stories men and women tell. Imagine
the thrill the locksmith must have felt,

crossing the threshold into a better life,
a secret he couldn't possibly keep, for as long
as it took to change the locks and leave. And on

the seawall, choices narrowing—imagine my friend
poised between action movie hero—all rage
and agency—or action film cliché,

another disposable girl. She takes to the air,
for frame upon frame upon frame,
her flight the surest kind of fighting.

On the Lam

Every July when I sat for an hour or so
in my grandparents' dismal single-wide, squeezed
on the couch between my mother and father,
my grandparents shouting questions at us,
not waiting for our answers, I wondered if life
was just a series of torments and obligations,

my grandfather going to war then working
as a plumber all those years only to land
in central Florida with nothing but the trailer, an RV
on busted tires, and little crystal animals
watching it all disintegrate from the shelves.
My grandmother's cousin Forrest, meanwhile,

was robbing banks in his sixties across the Southwest
with a crew cops called the Over-the-Hill Gang
—now that would have given us something to talk about
instead of whether I wanted to be a teacher
or a stewardess, the only options Grandma
could see for me before she went back to screaming

at her husband or my father, and I slipped off the couch
to study the family portraits in the hall.
There were my father's sisters, their boys, then me.
My grandmother's cousin excelled at finding opportunities,
marrying women under fictitious names,
devising more elaborate escapes—

eighteen in all—from each new jail, rowing
out of San Quentin in a kayak he'd built
in the prison shop. As for my grandparents,
they seemed to be on the lam from something too,
way out there in the woods where we got lost
each year, my parents arguing over

my father's hand-drawn map. Those summers I thought
I suffered alone, my parents having pledged
not to utter an unkind word about the trailer
or the people inside it, until I was twelve or so,
old enough to hear the truth, or some of it.
My parents left out the foster home, the worst

of the beatings, the floor of the garage
where my father slept beside the dogs, the rent
they charged him to sleep there. And still we went,
my father unable to loosen their hold,
the way his mother's cousin kept robbing banks
after he'd taken millions, as though he needed

prison for life to make sense. You may
have seen the movie about cousin Forrest,
Robert Redford playing him sexier and kinder
than could have been possible. In a year or two,
the Feds would close in on him back in Florida.
He'd be arrested again, then released,

then rob more banks, and die in prison, so maybe
the lesson is life is a series of disappointments
and then you die, or maybe sometimes you die
and an aging heartthrob buys the rights
to your story. I think it's almost funny now,
the way we huddled on that couch counting the minutes

until we could escape, yet here I am
again, probing the fights, the figurines,
the awful smells, and the way my face smiled down
from the cells of picture frames as though I were loved,
as though I were happy there—or maybe waiting
for the guards to turn their backs so I could run.

Combustibles

Pinto leaves you with that warm feeling.
     —tagline dropped from Ford radio ads

Even before I knew about the explosions,
the recalls, and the late-night television jokes,
or read the memo that measured the value of human life
and found it wanting, I had my own reasons to hate
my father's orange and white '73 Ford Pinto.

Already ugly when he'd bought it, seven years used,
for a hundred dollars, it suffered his benign neglect,
torn red cellophane fluttering across a taillight,
papers and cups collecting in every crevice, rust
spreading like mold, mold growing where it rained inside.

Riding in the backseat meant straddling a hole
in the floorboard, watching the asphalt tumbling by
through a latticework of rust. But worse than all of that
was that I sometimes rode to school—to middle school,
where students ranged in pimply throngs, scanning the crowd

for weakness. I made him drop me at the end of the block,
as though no one could see me there, and walked away
head-down, afraid of what the car said about me,
who I was, where I came from. For a year or so,
my father worked at a dealership on the side,

talking my classmates' parents into new convertibles
or cars for their older children's sweet sixteens. Each time
he came home, I hoped he hadn't mentioned me, the way
I hoped no one had seen me walk away from him
and the car as if I could leave my ugliness behind.

GLENIS REDMOND is the first Poet Laureate of Greenville, South Carolina. She is a 2023 Poet Laureate Fellow selected by the American Academy of Poets. Her latest books are *The Listening Skin* (Four Way Books) and *Praise Songs for Dave the Potter* (University of Georgia Press). Redmond received the Governor's Award and was inducted into the South Carolina Academy of Authors in 2022. *The Listening Skin* was shortlisted for the Open Pen America and Julie Suk awards.

Red Clay, as a Thread

Red clay, a thread, a promised pulse
running through and through.
If I listen, put my finger to the hum,
I can follow the story Mama tells
about when she was Little Nette
sent with a bucket and shovel
to the banks by her mama and aunts
to fetch clean clay.

I muse at the notion of dirt being clean,
but we are riddled with contradictions
of where we come from.

Mama, I can make you out,
how you heaped the lumps
and hauled them home
to cut into bite-sized pieces
to bake and dry.

I can see how the clay turned
mouths red as they munched
on the chunks.

How they hid the bounty
in tied flour sacks away
from the little ones
who, too, had acquired the taste.
Was it iron-poor blood?
No one ever said,
but the song does.
I know it was the blood.
I know it was the blood.
I know it was the blood for me.

I crave you too, not to eat,
but the sight
of your saturated color—
every time I walk or drive by
an excavation site,
you stand me still in hunger.
You make me know myself
in ways I cannot name,
but I feel you.

Even while watching a documentary
on African American foodways, *High on the Hog*,
you circle me like a shawl.
They flash to the road of no return,
but I have returned. Keep returning.
See your thread. Feel my ancestors' lift-off
the red clay ground,
the last land their feet touched
before boarding slave ships.
I feel a dizzying deficiency,
but still, you come and calm me.
Circle my home like Mama's hug,
a red clay and stone bed.
You hold every bulb and seed I plant.
Produce bright blooms and emerald shoots.
Everything I plant flourishes.
I become my foremothers—
not with thumbs,
but with the greenest hands.
I sow and sew their might to my own
with this perennial thread,
I quilt a living map
from what was meant
to unmake us.

There's No Sharing in Sharecropping

The crop's our clock, and our hands keep good time
move every which way in these heat-filled fields

from the morning moon to the setting sun
we bear the brunt of the bulk.

Shoulder and back into cotton
because cotton don't pick itself,

we do, but we don't own this land,
the landowner does.

Therefore, the landowner owns us.
Come harvest, we get no bounty.

He tells us we picked 100 bales,
but our backs know it's 300.

We, behind in this field and in life.
We, get the short end of every long row.

What the Auger Says

for Clayton Peg Leg Bates

The damage is done,
by my own twists and turns.
What could I do,
but keep going?
Not my will,
or want,
but by man's hand.

Finally, someone found him,
but the off-command
came too late.

I caught his left leg
and two fingers
on his right hand.

He got no business here,
but there he was
working the best he could.

When the lights went out.
He stepped into me.
I crushed bones
mashed and mangled flesh
cut like a hunter's breaking knife.
Blood everywhere!

Just 12 years old, he was
on his 3rd day at 3 am
at the cotton mill.

That boy's leg,
Became a terrible sight

and I was the site
of the scene,

I did not do it,
there's lots of blame
going 'round.
I get plenty of it.

If I could, I would've altered fate.
Before Clayton's hollers and pleas
sliced the night.

SUZANNE UNDERWOOD RHODES is a teaching poet and the Arkansas Poet Laureate. A native of New York, she lives in Fayetteville and has published several poetry collections, including the award-winning *Flying Yellow*. Her most recent collection is *The Perfume of Pain*, a chapbook published by Kelsay Books. Her poems, many of which have won awards, appear regularly in journals and anthologies such as *Shenandoah, Slant, Mid/South Anthology, Alaska Quarterly Review, Southern Poetry Review*, and *Image*. Rhodes taught creative writing and literature at King University and other colleges, and currently teaches virtual poetry workshops through the Muse Writers Center in Norfolk, Virginia. Believing with Kafka that poetry, like books, should be "an ax for the frozen sea within," she recently brought poetry workshops to the women residents (previously incarcerated) of Magdalene Serenity House in Fayetteville and published their creative works in a book, *Today There Have Been Lovely Things*.

Acknowledgments

"Cutting Hair"
> First appeared in *Image*

"Dorothy Bradford: A Very Grown Sea'"
> First appeared in *Spoon River Poetry Review*

"The Way My Grandmother Peeled a Potato"
> First appeared in *What a Light Thing, This Stone* (Sow's Ear Press, 1999)

Missing Persons

The finch's nest sprang up
one secret day in May
in my unguarded wreath.

I dared not disturb it,
a living story
embedded in my heart

whose guidance was,
don't come close,
check the mail some other way.

No one, not me nor you
(had you been here),
was allowed passage

through the door
with its window letting me
glimpse the play of shadows

and the hatchlings
dimly shifting,
their beaks crying

with hunger going back
to the beginning
of every child's

mother laboring
to nourish the trembling body
under her wings.

After weeks, the finches fledged.
All but one I found
when I took down the wreath,

a sad little rag
whose death was known
by the glare of day

who might, says my heart,
be alive in the air
where you are.

Cutting Hair

On the day to cut your hair
the sun has shaken
its shaggy mane of light
over the near ocean
over the trees behind our house
after a night of hunting
after birds have refilled the trees
and death has slipped
into the deep woods, its memory
scant as a snail's thread on the patio.

I wrap you in a cape and snug it with a clip.
How careful I must be, rounding
your good ear with scissors, the ear
my tongue loves to kiss, apricot-sweet,
and loves, too, the bad ear and its ghosts.
I thread your hair with a comb to gauge
length, silver in my loom.

I cut your hair in rhythm, remembering
the day you shaved what was left
of mine, how we walked
on a trail through the marsh, through
tufts of fog and I was slow as soup
of low tide, slow against your arm
remembering what it was like
not to lean, to be bright in my bones.

I see light differently now
painting the branches
behind our house, early, before
you're awake. It's more the gold
of afterlife, I think, a glimpse
before bodies take on all
that death.

Dorothy Bradford: "A Very Grown Sea"

Cradling my hand, cuffed in a ruffle,
he asked, would I cross the sea?

Candlelight spilled on the table,
lighting the plate of bones.

How could I know my own mind,
swayed by his hollow cheeks
and grave, bent shoulders?

Just as I never told
my love for patterned prayers
and painted glass that kept me safe
in the straits of a rote God who took no thought
for the brightly errant threads of a dreamer,

neither could I confess I had no faith
for the trip, would rather brave
the known foes of Leyden
than a gaping beyond.

For I have striven to live by Sarah's rule,
saying "Yes, I will follow after,"
binding my streaming hair in the bonnet,
shunning my prayer book hid in satin folds,

yielding my flesh to him but never voicing at all
the cries of buried tides for fear he'd think me
wanton like Strangers ever seeking
to draw us in, how I faltered at his throbbing hands

as I am faltering here in this hole
with the lantern swinging
and mothers and children doubled over,
the mountainous sea pitching us like a ball.

"Pukestocking," the sailors call us
and leer like devils. Oh,

I know they can see clear down
the well of my soul where I have kept
from him, even him, a dread
that gives way to strangely
painted thoughts not meet for one elect.

Often, I visit a lush banquet and taste,
but all is emptied, wasted in these waves

where I wish more than life
to fling my gray stocking
and lie in a dreamless hollow.

The Way My Grandmother Peeled a Potato

When she finished
there was one long
unbroken chain
coming off the body
like a soul.
She sang as she worked
and even had a hymn
for cutting the eyes out.

She wrung out her wash
same as chicken necks,
and when Grandpa died,
she went on making bread
for the empty place.

Once when I was little
she took me out to the cotton patch
and I watched her twist the beards off
those puckered faces and throw them
in her sack as she swung down her row,
her red bonnet loud as the sun
with me following,
wishing for hands like hers,
part man, part woman.
Then she gave me my own row
but the burrs cut my hands
and a sweat bee stung me
and I think she was sorry
I wasn't more help.

After I married
I marked her ways,
how she pieced her biscuit dough
and thickened pot liquor,
how she judged clouds

and knew the one to fly from,
huddling in the storm pit
with Grandpa and his light
until she reckoned the wind dead
and rose from the dark,
though the last storm
was her heart
and it carried her far.

I never could catch on
to her quilts and poultices
that patched what was severed,
but sometimes when I'm calling
the children, or beyond
to some fearful stillness,
I hear her sweeping up the stairs
like wind up a ridge,
big-boned and strong
to take me over.

Milk from the Moon

I can't seem to get past the stage
of hugging your shirt to my chest
like Daisy sobbing over Gatsby's shirts,
only your shirt has no money smell, just
the pure sweet body of you in the blink of time
where I live and you are not.

The ladder you climbed to the secret place
above the trees, the ladder propped against the oak
behind our house, with its wise old leaves
and songs within its branches blown away, away.
And the song from the stars, milk from the moon
gone too with you.

A heaven beyond moon or stars desired you
and owns you with infinite love that makes
my ache for you small as the coffee cup
with the snug-fitting handle your thumb liked,
and raw as my flawed, freckled body missing
the press of flesh that held us in the breach.

MONA LISA SALOY, Louisiana Poet Laureate (2021-2023), is an author, scholar, folklorist, Louisiana Folklife Commissioner, and educator of Creole culture in articles, documentaries, and poems about Black New Orleans before and after Katrina. She currently serves as Conrad N. Hilton Endowed Professor of English at Dillard University. Her book of poems, *Red Beans and Ricely Yours*, won the T. S. Eliot Prize and the PEN/Oakland Josephine Miles Award; *Second Line Home* celebrates New Orleans Black Creole culture. Recent publications include the *Chicago Quarterly Review*, *Black FIRE!!! This Time* anthology, *Tribes* journal NYC, and *Persimmon* journal. Her new collection *Black Creole Chronicles: Poems* (University of New Orleans Press 2023) was chosen for One Book One New Orleans 2024. Mona Lisa Saloy writes for those who don't or can't tell Black Creole cultural stories. Website: www.monalisasaloy.com. Tweet to @redbeansista.

Women Are Wonderful!!!

We are she her Eve
Sisters Mothers
Nanans Auntees Neighbors
My Sheroes our Sheroes
Girlfriends Nuns Teachers
Midwives saving new
Moms & new borns
Sojourners reaching her hands to
Help all she can
We are
Nurses Doctors a Vice President of the United States of America
standing on
Strong shoulders of a
Shirley who chiseled her way into
Talk of making our vote count then
Standing marching preaching the Good
We are the Fanny Lous
Sick & tired of seeing the same old
Ceilings blocking equal entry to professions to equal pay for work when
We do more just because we see need
Black Mothers 80% who die more than others
Their healthcare ignored behind the
Black veil still too strong after centuries
We are the Warrior Women the
Nefertaris the Queen Nzingas
Leading on the battlefield of life
We are women living to tell our tales so the
Lioness speaks before the hunter tells it wrong.

For My 7th Ward Warrior Women
for Mother

Mother became Catholic to marry Daddy. A PK (Preacher's Kid) herself, the eldest of six, from early used to helping at church, Mt. Zion Baptist Church on N. Robertson Street co-founded by her dad, she cleaned, bleached, washed pulpit and table linens for years, baked for church picnic sales, etc. Ensured we attended & helped. Then via marriage, a reverent Catholic, she did the same for Epiphany Priests, bleaching, starching, & pressing white vestments, altar cloths, Baptismal cloths for decades. Baked lemon cakes for events.

Mother walked New Orleans Streets, saving bus fare for us for shaved ice, ferry rides on Friday nights, for fundraisers to bury friends, or for Bid Whist games with neighborhood ladies like Mrs. Maugeritte Bradshaw, who washed and hot-pressed my wet nappy hair summers after swimming each day before Sunday church. Afraid of water, Mother made the sign-of-the-Cross every time I walked home from Hardin Pool across the street dripping wet, happy-faced smiling from a full day of Freestyle, Breaststroke, Backstroke, Butterfly-racing, or mermaid synchronized swimming, my heaven, her fear of water swallowing me.

Mother taught me to make perfectly-pleated skirts for the clothes-pin dresses, of left-over scraps thrown out from daily sewing Haspel Brother Seersucker Suits—the hallmark of Southern gentlemen. Those little dresses slipped onto wire hangers that adorned the clotheslines in our backyard to dry newly washed family clothes on red-beans-and-rice Mondays, 7th Ward wash day.

Too young yet to cook more than eggs & grits, or cut fresh lettuce, tomatoes, with thinly sliced onions for salad topped with olive oil, Mother taught me how to "blue" her pink hydrangeas with used coffee grounds, how to halt mice and rats from our yard planting wild mint around the edges.

On rainy days, we designed crochet doilies and sang Negro Spirituals—"Swing Low, Sweet Chariot"—and prayed-away storms beating our windows when the lights went out and the hurricane lamps lit our way like her faith and our family. For birthdays or holidays, Mother shared how to beautifully wrap a gift, the multiple-layered bows with curled ribbons cascading like rainbow waterfalls. Her Gumbo was better than Daddy's, more File, more spices than his.

One spring, she stopped everything, stayed in bed; her doctor baffled, since always active, healthy, she was sent to Flint Goodridge Hospital, the Negro Hospital, where they said cancer found her bones. Mother's beautiful ebony face went from chocolate to blue-black, in two weeks, and passed away, so we asked the Pastor to our home to pray with us, as Mother would have wanted. We sent word to the Priest. Me, two weeks past 16, in our living room of green wallpaper with black Egyptian motifs, a modern design, he told us that as children of two divorced parents remarried, we were mortal sin & should never have been born.

Thank God Cousin Glenn went around the corner to St. Augustine High School who sent his teacher-priest who came, comforted us, prayed with us, and confirmed that Mother could not be buried by the church, the Catholic Church who sanctioned enslavement of our ancestors for 600 years. I divorced Catholicism that day, not God, searching for a new church home for decades until returning to New Orleans and again worshiping with family at St. Raymond, where our Masses rock with Contemporary Gospel, Negro Spirituals, a comfort sustaining my culture and spirit.

Fall, 2022, when my brother Anthony's boyhood-neighborhood friend, Kenneth Evans, sat with me on the front gallery of our shotgun home finally rebuilt over a decade-and-a-half years since drowning in nine-and-a-half feet of water of post-Katrina flooding, he was planning a surprise 70th birthday party for lovely Tilly, his wife. Ok great! I was game to help. No, not why he came. Kenneth stopped by to tell me what he couldn't over the phone.

Kenneth said everyone in the neighborhood knew what the Priest told us that we should not have been born because our folks divorced.
What? I screamed. Who?
Neighborhood women he said, they were pissed! My eyes flooded now. Those women complained to the Archdiocese.
Who?
Mrs. Victoria Morrow lived in the 1919 shotgun built on St. Anthony Street.
Mrs. Victoria Evans, especially, and the other neighborhood women, fought for my Mother—that Priest was reassigned.
Kenneth's eyes watered with mine . . .

How does one thank Warrior Women no longer here for courage, selfless sacrifice, unsung efforts?

When I finally stopped crying, called my siblings still living—Tony, Barb, Sawa, shared Kenneth's revelation, we all stunned, shaking heads in shock.
Our eyes leaked all afternoon,

My heart at peace.
God answers prayers even
Prayers felt and unspoken.

Poem September Serenade

Cicadas sing early evening a
Concert before stars brighten
Dark skies of the hottest months
Since no one remembers, the
Symphony of cicada smiles
Beyond eyesight

JAN SEALE lives in McAllen, Texas, in the Rio Grande Valley. She is the author of ten poetry volumes and several books of short fiction and essays. Her writing has been featured in such venues as National Public Radio, the Dallas Museum of Art, and *Texas Monthly*. Her latest book of poetry is *Particulars: poems of smallness*. Forthcoming are *Elder Skelter* and *Border Biome*. Seale has taught writing at three universities and has held a National Endowment for the Arts fellowship in creative writing. She served as the 2012 Texas Poet Laureate and holds the Texas Poet Laureate title for life.

Acknowledgments

"Gentle Conversation"
        First published in *Blue Mesa Review*
"Eating Texas"
        First published in *Texas Poetry Calendar* 2010
"Mesquite Bean Coffee vs. Arabian Coffee" and "At the Museum of South Texas History"
        First published in *www.texaspoetryassignment.org*

Eating Texas

It's taken a long apprenticeship
to make waffles in the shape of Texas.
First there were mountains over Waco.
Then the Panhandle sank.

A few more false starts when
the Red River swamped Oklahoma
and the Rio Grande dripped into Mexico.
Now I can make perfect ones.

All I have to do is take care
to stop pouring the batter a little shy
of El Paso, Dalhart, and Texarkana.
For some reason, Brownsville needs more.

Otherwise, my grandchildren complain they
don't have the tail of Texas to bite off.

Gentle Conversation

My grandmother was named Malinche.

     Mine was named Melinda.

My mother was frightened by a lunar eclipse.

     My mother ate too many pickles and strawberries.

Once I was almost killed by a flying tortilla.

     I was seriously grazed by a slice of white bread.

My family had a *porción* from the King of Spain.

     My family had a bunk on the Mayflower.

I spent my childhood in the *campo*.

     I spent my childhood on a vacant lot.

My maiden name is Garza.

     My maiden name is Jones.

My married name is Garcia.

     My married name is Johnson.

I am the color of nutmeg.

     I am the color of cream.

Mesquite Bean Coffee vs. Arabian Coffee

Why would you do this, take a holy
popular elixir and borrow its name?

      Who said coffee must be made
      with a strict heritage from Africa?

Why not call mesquite bean coffee
Mesquite-aide or Bean Consommé?

      Why call your coffee Transfusion,
      Jitter Juice? Java? Joe?

But couldn't this go trending, spreading
to pinto or lima or green pea coffee

      Is there a license, a copyright
      for black, comforting, exotic?

. . . maybe sneaking on to carrot coffee,
radish coffee, tomato coffee?

      Oh come now, aren't we getting
      a bit defensive and upset?

But what does it look like, this sipped
stuff before it is brewed?

      If you must know, like fine sand,
      with a few twigs, mere shreds.

Has anyone asked permission to grind beans
and pods, offer the resulting concoction?

      Could you stop making distinctions,
      just be open-minded and tolerant?

Liquid trash trees! Cow feed! That's what it is!
Vaqueros out on the range with *nada* else.

> Look: It isn't against the law,
> heretical, unhealthy, or misnamed.

No stimulant? Depression could set in,
upending the universe, stopping civilization.

> Here. Calm yourself. Take a sip.
> Consider it a peace offering.

The Lesser Rio Grande Siren

S. i. texana

Put your hands together
for this snake-like salamander,
one with front legs only,
with frilly gills and no eyelids.
He's highly secretive, lives in mud,
vocalizes clicks and screeches.
He might stretch out two feet long.

He's our own Texas treasure,
before our state, before Mexico,
before the Aztecs, and all those
before, including dinosaurs.
His folks date 230 mil years ago.

Not a mockingbird or armadillo,
not bluebonnet blue or pecan tasty,
still he's ours, so ours, and
we have the sense
to love him as Endangered.

At the Museum of South Texas History

Step into the main gallery, second floor:
a mammoth from the Pliocene epoch
trumpets silent welcome, and overhead
an ichthyosaurus churns the Paleo-Gulf.

Move to the diorama: smooth Coahuiltecans
bring a wild turkey back to camp
while cicadas chirp and a jaguar growls.
These humans are carefully not leaving
a written record, only shell fragments,
chipped stone flakes, campfire hearths.

Next, Spaniards in helmets and chain mail
lead horses through the thorn scrub forest,
trample the prickly pear cactus.
Now civilization commences near fresh water,
with colonists hanging church bells,
electing *alcaldes*, plowing the fields.
In a narrow *jacal*, an Aztec descendant
sings quietly, tells a mythical tale of a lover.

A rattlesnake menaces, a cook brews
coffee from mesquite beans. Across,
an entrepreneur checks his steamboat
for passage on the Rio Grande.
Meanwhile, downstairs the greeter
readies the computer, the cash box,
the visitor bracelets. The building
supervisor flings open oak doors,
lets in sunlight for a brief air-out.
The gift store lights flash on.

A bobcat strolls in.

(This museum is not in the suburbs.
This museum is no kitschy tourist attraction.
MOSTH boasts a board, a website,
an archive, national listing; has won prizes,
is solvent, imposing, sits on the square
opposite the county courthouse.)

The bobcat steps lively, bringing
a lovely buff color, with spots,
long legs, fuzzed feet, facial ruffs, ear tufts,
gleaming eyes, porcelain pink nose,
and, topping it off, a short curled-up tail—
all these declaring it is not Tabby Americana.

The bobcat looks about, startled at shrieks
and running feet. Perhaps it is wondering
where water is, where chipmunks, where snakes.
It turns, and on retractable claws moves quietly
from the stone tiles of the entryway to the gift store.

Full of purpose, it heads straight
for the book display, (ahh, our kind of cat!)
climbing shelf by shelf to the top, turning,
checking its vantage, settling in a corner.
Was it once an Egyptian cat on a tomb?

Exhibit A licks its paws, takes a spit bath
after the long journey to town. Then settles.
Here we see a learned cat, a scholarly feline,
an educated carnivorous mammal,
a book lover cat having chosen to preside over
The Amazing Life of a South Texas Cowboy,
The Rio Grande Delta and *I'd Rather Sleep in Texas*.

In true reverence to the region's biome,
the police are not called, only Animal Control.
These folks, delighted, relieved of boring stray dogs,
do a careful takedown, feline to opossum cage.

Upcountry, "Hello," yells the rancher into his phone,
"A WHAT you say?" He knows all about MOSTH,
believes in heritage, history, this peculiar land.
So he gets in his pickup, drives an hour into town,
stomps into the museum, kneels and looks
into shining yellow eyes.

"Well hello hello, Betty Bobcat," he croons.
With a name, she's taken up, walked to the door.
She's over the side of his pickup; to home on his range.
So much for show-and-tell, for a live demonstration.
So much for not-musty, not-dead museum displays.
Here's to living history. Yowl! Pssttt!

ROY SEEGER moved to Aiken, SC, in 2008 where he teaches poetry courses in the University of South Carolina Aiken's BFA in creative writing program. His collections include *The Boy Whose Hands Were Birds*, winner of the 2008 *Main Street Rag* Poetry Contest, and *Prayerbook for the Midwestern Agnostic*. His poetry has been anthologized in *Archive: South Carolina Poetry Since 2005* and has appeared in various journals including *Jasper*, *Gulf Coast*, *32 Poems*, as well as others. He is the recipient of the 2018 Carrie Nickens McCray Fellowship from the South Carolina Academy of Authors.

Bird Shit Good Luck

Since it is spring in Aiken again,
we mark the season's passing
by the barely ripe blackberries
that pass through local birds,
seeding the yard until brambles
threaten the ivy, the lawn, the bottoms
of my seasonally tender feet.
And one shoot finds
the right conditions
on the hood of my old, pitted Honda,
sets root in the rust and grime.
And of course, it will never bear fruit,
but there it is, digging
impossible roots
into a patch on the hood,
and when I drive
the local roads to the grocery,
the zealous shoots
keep their precarious hold.
And I swear they lengthen as they flap
in the wind—graceless things
with a futile and otherwise thorny nature.

Whenever I Dance, I Imitate John Travolta

After cutting the encroaching trees
and splitting the trees we burn
the neatly stacked wood
in the stove all the way
through May sometimes while
the copper kettle, refilled with water
daily, reintroduces the moisture
fire draws from air. This
is my father's house;
he is in the very woodwork;
he saturates even the dust, and me
alone, with the window open wide,
letting the heat out and,
of all things, dancing. Nobody home
and Roy dancing, dancing to no rhythm,
to no particular music, dancing,
television on and muted,
dancing. This is nothing
I'd ever teach my children, nothing
they couldn't learn themselves:

plant the toe and twist the leg;
point to the sky, point to the ground;
don't look where you are pointing.

The Split-Headed Frog of Double-Consciousness

With the consistency of an unbaked
sweet potato, my smallest finger
is circumcised by the heavy knife,
bringing new awareness of the difference
between finger and not finger.

Before the deep red blood welled
past the skin flap, in the minutes
before my vision tunnels, I
remember all the frogs of my life,
loose in the kitchen.

And when the butcher's knife split
the frog's head, it looked
like a cartoon cigar exploding.
Then it jumped off the cutting board,
barely noticing its sagging change
in perspective.

Had the knife been sharp enough
and the cut true enough,
the frog might have lived as two halves.
And would each miss the other
in these separate lives?
Be drawn to the symmetry of the self
seeking a mirrored self?
Lay side by side and pretend to be whole?

Then I remember my finger,
wrapped in a paper towel and clutched
in a frantic futile stopping-of-blood gesture,
and I think of the individual
blood cells spilling out of my finger,
until I am a single red cell rushing
through my own veins and out
into this new atmosphere.

And then I physically fall—
I think of the flap
of skin still attached to my thumb
and I already miss it.

I think it might do fine without me—
a new fragment of consciousness
that would devote itself completely to itself.
I am jealous.

Synapses fire in all directions.
Missed connections, missed connections.
And the split-head frog jumps left.
And the split-head frog jumps right.
We're all already dead and just don't know it.

Poem in Which the Safe-Word
Is Reader Response Criticism

When puppy is being bad, all
the training books advise,
hold down firmly until wiggling stops
and puppy lets out a large sigh,
a sure sign of submission—
Consider the context of this sigh
as the turdish thing she just rolled in.
There's no ignoring it.
There's no putting it out of your mind.
There are some interactions
that must never occur in polite society,
and when they do, the only
response is to shower afterwards.
But remember when our bodies
sang in the pitch dark? (or did
they laugh?) La ha ha!
Then we fell asleep in a tangle.
And afterwards came celebrities
with their head-
lines and night vision goggles!
A million American teens turn
to their computer screens
in search of puberty!
Then, as if in conspiracy, a nation
of dogs scratch
at the door to be let out.
And this is how we meet, comp-
lamenting each other's dogs
while they urinate on a neighbor's
rhododendrons—
connections, connections, every-
where connections
despite what we do to isolate ourselves.
Get online and blog about it!

What did your teacher
mean by *cheese* and the *cutting* of it?
Develop three possible theories
by Monday. Choose
a font to express the core
of your inner creative self. Meanwhile,
you can almost hear the instruction
of cursive writing fade from grade school
curriculums across the country.
And this is the trouble
with communication—
language always in flux—hip joint,
fur muff, cut the cheese, cut
the cheese, cut the
cheese. I say what Stanley
Fish says, except I say it
knowing what I know about
my father, how he ends up.
The text in the classroom
is the text of the body
in the act of reading, which is a form
of creation. And just remember this—
whoever penned "a sigh is just
a sigh" was working to get everybody laid.
And the record player goes thump, thump, thump.

Amanda's in the Backyard, Plucking at the Banjo

The banjo knows one history of sorrow—
in the cat-gut strings & crisp twang of its body.

The back porch on Rollingwood was alive with false starts,
                    with the process of process.

Your fingers speed up time,
bring all them old times back 'round—and out

of the banjo's steel rim and frosted head emerged the things
you regretted missing out on when you were young—

call them "You Are My Sunshine," call them
                    "Boil them Cabbage Down."

The history beneath these moments—call it "comfort"
(which, in the perfect Bluegrass song,

                    would rhyme seamlessly with "lament").
And each evening settles around our backyard like a refrain.

        And the only song that I can sing is
        Boil them cabbage down.

The backyard lit up with your temporary persistence.

MARTHA SERPAS has written four volumes of poetry, including *The Dirty Side of the Storm* and most recently *Double Effect*. A native of Bayou Lafourche, Louisiana, she co-produced *Veins in the Gulf*, a documentary about land loss in the Barataria-Terrebonne Estuary. She teaches at the University of Houston and co-directs Scripts, the narrative and lyric health program at UH's Tilman J. Fertitta Family College of Medicine. She is a hospital trauma chaplain and a recent graduate of the Berkeley Center for the Science of Psychedelics' psychedelic facilitation program.

Acknowledgments

"Grand Isle Invocation" and "Fragments of the Sacrificial World"
    First published in *Plume*
"Conversion"
    From *Côte Blanche* (New Issues Press)
"Just Call Me *Beb*"
    From *Double Effect* (LSU Press)
"The Best of Us"
    From *The Diener* (LSU Press)

Grand Isle Invocation

Park near the cemetery
where there is a playground and picnic tables.
Some of the best birds of the day have been seen here while
eating lunch.
                    —Orleans Audubon Society

The warblers, vireos and thrushes fall out
            their three-day spring-break drunk
            into oak   and hackberry   They've stopped to see

if the island is still dying and since it is
            they continue on . . .
            (I too can be seen here   misplaced . . .)

Before I die a single live oak will catch
            their exhaustion   They will cubby
            like high-tops hung from the Loneliest Road

in America   They will sing the LSU fight song
            and take the 18-hour flight   the red-eye
                        back to Cancún

Conversion

The tracks got ripped up like a busted zipper,
thrown down, piles of tar and broken ties,
into the dead grass on the bayouside.

You have to understand: only time tears things
down here. Long after you quit a house, pack
up and leave, that house stands

Catalogued, under sheets of rust, paneless,
porchless, for years. Cast-iron kettles
won't move, won't be moved,

The air above their bellies, still and sharp.
No one remembers the cane they boiled
or how they came to kill grass

Where they do. Half an old bridge
makes a sweet fishing spot—but taking
the rails away, it was an insult, really,

A theft. I saw how one loss collapses
into another, the rings between them,
almost indistinguishable.

But then, to the right of the road,
the shoulder leapt with sunflowers,
the blue sky dangled like a scarf,

And the part of me that was buried
came back like the dead after hard rain,
just pushed up the glass lid

And stepped onto solid ground. Backwater rises
to its own schedule, covers the highways,
you can't tell the bayou's banks

From the road's edge, and then there's no question
of staving off conversion.
Even the dead won't be held down.

Just Call Me *Beb*

>   *for Joy at the Baton Rouge Best Buy*

Just call me *beb.*
Just lift more than one finger
off the steering wheel when we pass
each other in the 25, my having
assumed I could use your lane
to get around the cane truck,
and your grill smiling
like a wildcat coming on.
Just call me *beb*, like
when you put down my catfish
po-boy having told me
it was just filleted in the back
that morning and then
putting a *lagniappe* of two strips
in front of my friend who ordered
the Plate Lunch instead.
Beb, you said, *it's reeeally good.*

Sometimes joy has to be pushed
on me, like when I tried
to cancel my order online
and then had to call the store
and I got you, Joy, and you
called me *beb* and we talked
about computers and breast cancer
and that talk you had with God
on your way home from the Lowe's
parking lot where you got your scan.
Just don't let me whine, you said,
'cause nobody likes a whiner,
and if God said anything, God said,
Beb, I liked you from the first.

*It was the best thing that ever happened
to me*, you said.

I should call myself *beb* every day, and I
wonder, if I knew I was going to be reborn,
whether I wouldn't grieve extra hard
because there is Life and there is This Life
and I'd have to give up hope
for this one, the hope that some further
saving possibility could be found here,
and then wait to catch a warm front
and fly away to the next one, well, then I might
be like you, Joy, listening for the rustle
of palmetto leaves in the dark
as I put my steps down on the path,
the bebettes harmonizing after the rain.

The Best of Us

Give me your Greek myths
and I'll give you the Carmen

Kief Bridge—forgotten,
whatever it was called before—

where thirty years ago Trey
scaled the steel lift

still hot from the sun of the day,
with a spray can under his chin,

to inscribe the I-beam with the promise
of her memory and the imprimatur of his passion.

Or when Oris Lee did his girlfriend on the front lawn
at lunch—I was speechless with admiration.

The football coach looked him right in the eye
and Oris looked right back. The coach, hardly

able to draw his smile or keep his hand from pounding
Oris on the back as if he were a safety

just trotting off the field with his first interception.
(What girl could I hold—even under the bleachers?)

Trey sat with his brother on the T-top
of their Trans Am, a big, wing-stretched

bird stamped in gold on the hood.
They drank the better of a twelve-pack

under the scrawl of a new constellation.
There was no moon, there was no call.

Mr. Kief went to early Mass
with his wife and four daughters,

auburn muses sliding into his car,
one hotter than the next, down to his baby girl,

whose breasts even the straight girls attended.
Did Carmen see the blazón first or did her father,

driving with his neck stretched as if
the crimson letters themselves were suitors

tearing up his sod and eating at his table?
Before the sun set, sandblasters were at work

clouding the message and blotting the sword.
Fathers themselves, they scrubbed

the rust patches and rivets almost to clouds, like those
around great mountain peaks, red rocks

and crags reaching through too-visible haze. "Trey"
watered down to foam by the gritty spray, "loves"

running in faint streaks, but "Carmen" flaring
like the night it was born from Trey's nozzle.

All that Mr. Kief could not rid himself of:
how his baby became the protagonist,

how she acted through the actor, freeing
herself through photon bonding at the head

of this, our gateway bayou. Shame is such
a bastard, its fly-by-night parents,

338

cowardice and hubris—all that we know
better than God, all we hide from the grass

and the sky. *Her* name will be remembered,
not like a trophy or the blotted girl on the lawn

but like a woman who guards the pass
or a woman who starts a war.

Fragments of The Sacrificial World

Porpoises feed every morning in the shallows
it's hard to tell tail from fin   even
      on flatwater

My dog belly-up scratches her back on some pelican froth
at the hightide line   hard to tell snout from tail

She finds dead things in the rough
a joie this morning we share

A fleet of white pelicans seems somewhat acquainted
with the porpoises' drill
in an indifferent kind of way
in a we're-really-not-looking-for-a-hand-out
kind of way

And if I think a shrimp eel has written my name in the sand there's
always
ecotheory and the justified tide   to set me right

Weather   and the rough disappears and
          per se and   absence tangles me
   the rough recedes
the rough covers the levee
the rough disappears

Twenty-one white jewels pinned
to the seam of the gulf   a frayed watchpocket
a long hem   wind that won't lay down

JOHN WARNER SMITH was the Poet Laureate of Louisiana from 2019 to 2021 and is the only African American man to serve in the office in its eighty-two-year history. Smith has published five collections of poetry. His novella, *For All Those Men: When the KKK Threatened to Take Control of Louisiana,* was published by UL Press in November 2022. A Cave Canem Fellow, Smith is a 2020 Poets Laureate Fellow of the Academy of American Poets and is winner of the 2019 Linda Hodge Bromberg Literary Award. Smith earned his MFA at the University of New Orleans.

Dreams of the Shadows

for Pat Kahle

Bayou water, sugar land,
letters, ledgers,
photographs and paintings,
furnishings, clothing, and knickknacks,
histories told and untold
at the mansion on the bayou.

Here, in the South, in Iberia,
we bear witness to the beauty and brokenness of humans,
      the free ones who traded and profited
      and the captive, chattel ones
      who sweetened the salty earth beyond us,
      all hidden in the canopies
      of our draping moss and beckoning boughs.

In the whirling winds of centuries and seasons,
we bore seeds wing-borne and carried far away,
                    in air
whispering the *coo-woo* calls of mourning doves
and shouting the holy-danced *hallelujahs*
of freedom songs.

When twilight dimmed the cabins
and patterns were cut and stitched,

      we dreamt patches
      of fine lace and coarse cloth,
      a collage of crystal and glass,
      porcelain and cracked pottery,
      carved wood and bleeding hands.

Now, as sunbeams pierce the clouds,

we dream the mosaicked and unpainted,
the marbled and bare,
the privileged and poor,____disparate, yet,
forever bound together   by love.

When truth slumbers and dies
in the deep, dark well of memory,
we live, we remember, we tell.

See.   Listen.   Dream with us!

Rock of Ages
(On the 250th Anniversary of America)

Like jagged rock weathered by time,
severed and separated from a mountain,
the history of racial injustice in America
rolls slowly down the mossy slope.

Slavery   Civil War   Reconstruction

Jim Crow   KKK lynching   long gone.

No more Connor, Wallace, Helms, and Duke.

No killings of Civil Rights leaders.

No remorse in the national conscience.

Yet, the old weathering rock creeps along,
        pulled by the gravity of denialism,
                carving a path of flinty earth
        trodden with resistance and protests.

Not seen from the valley far below____
        a steep winding trail, cobbled
                with hardship and suffering,
        always in need of warmth and light.

Many with strength to endure
the mountain's daunting, rugged terrain,
some daring enough to look down
and back while climbing,

but few will reach the mountaintop,
unless our fears smolder in soul-lit fires,
and we walk the rough, widening path
of struggles for human rights and dignity.

Contemplation

You sense the faint whisper
growing closer and louder,

something alive, alluring,
yet threatening,

lurking behind a shut door
or an opaque window,

or inside a gleaming star,
something of spirit,

fallen from the sky
or sprung from earth,

thoughts old and darkening,
something of death

and questions unanswered,
like an avalanche

careening too fast,
an ache you cannot bear,

a hunger for light,
a heart needing love.

Watching God Recreate the Moon

Where I sleep, daylight peeps
through window blinds every morning,
bringing a day I haven't seen.

Hours later, as I sit
where the sun doesn't set
and ponder the weight of living,
ballpark lights gleaming in the distance
make the cheering and yelling
at children grow louder.

Late on this hot, humid night,
I watch a handless brush spatter paint
onto the blank, black sky.

Listening to inner thoughts
and the intrusive sound
of tires streaking across an asphalt road,
I am pulled inside the canvas,
finding the moon
rising with each blink and breath,
swallowing darkness
as it careens across the abyss,
engulfing the world below.

Nothing else exists,

no land, no humans, no sound,
nothing needed, wanted or feared____

only the surest, most absolute truth.

Deliverance

When his sales pitch shifted gears
and started to reach
smoothly into my wallet and bank account,
the used car salesman said,
Cars are just metal, plastic, and cushion____
meant only for utility.
People put too much heart into them.
I thought to myself, *horseshit.*

My compulsion to think repeatedly
about a barely noticeable spot
that hours and days of polishing couldn't remove
on the roof of my car
made the smell of his pitch hardly noticeable.

The more I looked and listened,
the more I heard a familiar Sunday sermon,
and like Jesus, blow mold,
and a prayer candle,
his little car started to glow
until, finally, I saw deliverance.

Georgia-born **RON SMITH**'s *Running Again in Hollywood Cemetery* was judged by Margaret Atwood "a close runner-up" for the National Poetry Series Open Competition; the book was recently issued in an enhanced edition by MadHat. Former Poet Laureate of Virginia, Smith has published four books with LSU Press: *Moon Road, Its Ghostly Workshop, The Humility of the Brutes*, and *That Beauty in the* Trees. His poems have appeared in numerous periodicals and anthologies, including *The Nation, Kenyon Review, Georgia Review, Southern Review*, and *Helen Vendler's Poems, Poets, Poetry*. Smith has been a presenter at more than a dozen international conferences and has read his poems on Virginia history and landscape at Mount Vernon, the Virginia House of Delegates, and the Virginia Senate, as well as Italy-inspired poems at Rome's Keats-Shelley House and the American Ambassador's residence, and pieces reflecting on literary modernism at the American Library in Paris—and to Hemingway scholars on the Eiffel Tower.

Acknowledgments

"Running Again in Hollywood Cemetery," "Railroad Track," "Water Tower," "Gatlinburg," "Declaiming," and "Katie on Her Education"
    From *Running Again in Hollywood Cemetery*, 2nd edition, by MadHat Press, 2020.

Running Again in Hollywood Cemetery

December, Richmond, Virginia

Nothing's changed here
since you and I climbed the sagging
chain link and honeysuckle
off Cherry St. to sprint the steep hills
of the dead. We knew what we wanted:
granite thighs for trampling linemen,
legs that could launch us over the caged faces
to break the plane between us
and gold figures we envisioned marching
across our mantels; women whose red lips
glistened and parted for everything
we could give them.

Coach ordered hills
so we ran here in a pumping race to this crest
where we stomped two presidents
with our breakdown drills,
where this stained woman still bends
a face I will never see into her metal hands.
Neither falling behind, we took each other
on a tour of lies, past the white slab
where you laid Sandy and showed your ass
to a screaming widow who lashed you bloody
with a dozen roses while you by God
went on and finished,

past the filth-eyed angels
drooping with sorrow, shrouded obelisks
and artfully broken columns,
sandstone tree trunks carved intricate
with rot, the gothic Randolph tomb
where I crowbarred the bronze
one August afternoon on Laura's dare,
where the west window broke the darkness

349

into colors over her shivers, and she laid back,
the Virgin's blue cloak across her scar
and my chest war painted,

and she said, I'm safe,
and I didn't believe her and spilled my seed
in Randolph's deep-carved name.
Which were the lies? Was the heavy door
already open? Did I really pour myself
into that gray stone? In the locker room your skinny ass
never had a scratch that I remember.
And what do we have now? Your Saturday
headlines have shrunk to one small name
in black marble not far from Lincoln's huge,
tired eyes in that other capital we cursed
with our simple history.

Alone in Vermont ice
I've tried to chase it all down,
pound some sense into it, like the time
I bloodied knuckles on Jeff Davis's cold jaw
and then on you because you thought
my whiskey meanness was Yankee sacrilege.
In the blinding light at breakfast we blamed
our bloody shirts and fist-changed faces
on the Church Hill boys.

Since then I've run
more miles than you ever ventured from home,
even for that jungle assault when
you came up vapor just before
your first R&R. They went back and back
for a week after pushing past that blasted clearing.
Nothing, not a dog tag, not a silver filling.
In the only letter you ever finished
you wrote of another city you never laid eyes on,
dreamed of yellow-faced women waiting
to set you on fire with
American diseases.

Today, lean for distance,
I have circled all the unchanging dead
with only a little chest burn, chasing
my breath up and down every hill I could find.
The pencil-necked guard who scared us away
in '65 is white-headed now, and almost fat.
He still chains the gate at sundown.
As early gold takes the Confederate pyramid
and every plinth and angel, a couple, arm in arm,
is walking on the flaming river far below.
I turn back for the granite arch
while there is still time.

Railroad Track

I sling my shoes to the edge of the yard
behind the house my father sold
to people I've never met
and go to feel the roughness of splintered ties
through the bare, thin soles of the present.
Between these rails, behind this house,
I am always an only child,
following this old spur
where a daydream nearly killed me once.

On this short line to the pulpwood plant
flatbeds rolled, throbbed our door frames
twice a day, chasing a horn
everybody said could raise the dead.
I bent for the blackberries' tiny grenades,
Hollywood bombs singing in my skull.
A man in a ratty garden was pointing,
his mouth open round
words that would not travel—

                    and the silence
went inside out, shook my chest with something
there all along and I turned to a
locomotive front like the wall of an iron cathedral,
a gargoyle engineer hanging from the sky, his face
twisting soundless curses, and a breath
before my legs melted I stepped
beyond the rails and the train,
the pitch of its howl dropping,
passed.

      In the quaking rocks close
to the shine of steel where wheel meets rail
like a razor on a metal strop,
I knelt until the pines came back

to the other side of the track and I could hear
mocking birds squabbling in the bushes
and the shrieks of girls far away
skipping rope safely in the street.

"You all right?" the old man called
from a row of stunted corn.
The rail joints clicked and clicked.
"Sure," I said. And I rose
from the sting of river rocks
and tightroped the smooth silver home,
bowing that night before a steaming plate
in the soft chant of Mother's usual blessing,
hearing none of the words
and all of the tired low promise of protection.

Water Tower

for Stan Tretiak

The wind behind us pulled on our packs.
Hands firmly on each steel rod, we were careful
to show we were never careful, even when
the ladder left the huge bolted leg to lean
for the catwalk circling above us like Saturn's rings.
A hundred feet above the streetlight
we unloaded blankets, bananas, and rum crooks.
Clenching our teeth on sweet tobacco,
we thought we had left town already.
Our dark neighborhoods at our feet,
the black sky strewn with close blue stars,
we matched nickels on the very top
and pulsed wholly red with warning
to pilots they were still too near the earth.

Our parents thought we hugged the ground
in the gnat-buzzing woods.
But even mosquitoes couldn't reach us up there.
Police Chief Crowder moved below us
in his slow square car, prowling the streets' angles,
throwing his yellow beam into the usual darkness
behind the Webbers' cinder block garage, under
the Methodist preacher's hedges.

We slept on the catwalk along the curve of steel,
and seven of us, toe to head,
could surround the whole town's water.
We rose full of water in the dawn, shivering,
hanging long pisses to the familiar street,
trembling stiffly, quickly down the cold rungs,
while dogs harangued the milkman
and the big trucks over on 17
made their hollow sounds passing through.

Gatlinburg

Beyond the cheese balls a man
the size of a lemon slice
is casting for trout.

His feet throb with the cold.
The Cabbage Patch woman drinks him
then goes back to the salad bar.

You have just told me to by God fuck off.
Everything on my plate is green
under the fluorescent lights.

You chew a line deeper
into the corner of your mouth.
The yellow slicker and black boots

move out of sight below us
then reappear to my right, downstream.
Cast and cast. The room is aquamarine.

The fisherman licks his tiny chapped lips
and looks right at you.

Declaiming

When my father takes my poems
in his fight-broken hands,
he holds my few words
at arm's length,
raises his rich, unused voice,
and calls each syllable
so carefully you can see
him declaiming Bryant
fifty years ago, at attention
beside his lunch pail
in the single room of Stilson School.

There, his cheeks are full of blood,
and he is handsome.
Parris Island is two years north.
He smells like the cows he milked
in the early Georgia dark.
He moves down each row
of phrases with the grimness
of those who feel
they must make the earth yield
its sweet corn,
its crouching Japanese,
catching up against
hard roots, going on

up the burning islands of the Pacific,
peering into the flaring dark
of each step north.
Against beachhead sunsets he sees
the Zeros sputter and go down.
In foxhole after foxhole he dreams
of dusty fields where he falls
behind the mule
and the rows close over him

and he comes up changed,
atabrine yellow,
wavering in the merest breeze,
his body whispering.

The days have gathered
into straight lines behind him.
After half a century
of the silent heft of steel
he is left with a handful
of someone else's words,
words that slip
between thick, crooked fingers
like the lightest of seeds.

Katie on Her Education

I went down to the river to walk,
to hear all those tons of water
the earth lured down from Virginia hills
the way you lured me,
and in the middle of the clay path
I met the man who'd taught me
how to think after you had
taught me how to feel.

He was with a woman
not his kindly coffee-bringing wife.
And his face was raw with guilt.
And his eyes were jerky with lies.
"Hello, Katie," he said in a gathering bass.
"We were trying to decide
what kinds of birds those are,"
he said, Dr. Warner, who taught me
Ethics, who demanded such care
with words, said.

In the huge, white-dead tree
were huge, black-still birds.
"Crows, I believe," I said.
Everybody knows crows.
Her face was white as the tree
and the water-rounded rocks.
We smiled a stiff set of smiles.
And then he led her away.

One day when we have not fought
I'll take you there
to walk the river's run,
to let you know I know just where
the crows along the river roost
and why.

LARRY D. THOMAS, the 2008 Texas Poet Laureate and a member of the Texas Institute of Letters, has published twenty-three print collections of poems and numerous poetry chapbooks, both in print and online. Of Southern heritage, he has dedicated his writing and publication efforts during the past few years to work either set in the American South, especially the Mississippi River Delta region, or work involving Southern culture. Thomas has been a regular contributor of poetry and fiction to a number of Southern journals, which include the *Arkansas Review: A Journal of Delta Studies, Deep South Magazine, Delta Poetry Review, Valley Voices: A Literary Review, Louisiana Literature, Green Hills Literary Lantern*, and *Red Dirt Forum.*

Ritual

(the vicissitudes of Houston "trash trees")

Each morning, I open the blinds for sunlight.
The upstairs window overlooks two Chinese tallows
joined at the ground like Siamese twins
decades beyond the death-promised option of surgery.

They spend their days glorified by the feet of birds,
squirrels, and the occasional nighttime descent
of rats exiting sagging freeways of electrical wires.
All year long I pick up after them, bundling

fallen branches, raking desiccated inflorescences
in the Spring, and clearing the driveway
of seeds the birds couldn't reach. Most of the neighbors
loathe and curse them, but I brook their constantly

raining trash for nothing but the yellows,
reds, burgundies and oranges which,
for a few short days toward the end of autumn,
vivify the solace of redemption.

Sewer Rats

(French Quarter, New Orleans, at dusk)

At dusk, after the sidewalks
have capitulated to the reign of shadow
and the streetlamps start flickering

in a purgatory neither day nor night,
they emerge. From my vantage point
three stories above, I think they are cats

the way they squeeze their corpulence
through the bars of sewer drains, so fat
they wobble down a concrete carpet

anything but red, dragging hairless tails.
They have a swagger to their gait,
stopping here and there to sniff

wads of trash before proceeding
down their esplanade of gutter
like the grisly floats of a coronation,

shoving the dark arrogance of their noses
smack in the face of public safety,
regal in the trappings of their filth.

Wild Boar

(Alabama backwoods)

He sports along his back
a sharp ridge of bristle.
His great-great-grandfather,

and he only for the days
it took to gain enough weight
to break the slats of his pigpen

like matchsticks, was the last
of his fabulous bloodline
to languish in the tedium

of domesticity. He owns
the backwoods and knows it.
His tusks gleaming in the moonglow

are perfect for grubbing roots
or, if need be, disemboweling
the hounds of drunk hunters.

Though his grunts are the Latin
of kids, this big fellow
goes anything but "wee, wee, wee"

all the way home. Even his sow
stands the starless night on edge,
grunting on her bed of crushed piglets.

Portuguese Men-of-War

(Atlantic coast, Florida)

Their muscular, gas-filled sacs
of blues, pinks and delicate,
beguiling lavenders

gleam in morning sun
like the nacreous,
sea-washed remnants

of shipwrecks.
Like floating angels
letting down their hair

in clouds, they dangle
their lengthy tentacles
in the green, translucent sea.

By the hundreds
they rise and fall,
far as the eye can see.

Their kindest touch
is injury, death
or blindness.

Wet Suit

(January, Tybee Island, Georgia)

After tugging it over
my shivering limbs
like a close-fitting glove
and zipping it up,
I clench my lips and gasp

as the sea seeps in
at my neck, wrists and ankles
and, warmed by my body heat,
forms a thin layer of insulation
between my skin and the rubber,

the sea which insulates me
the same sea whose cold can kill,
the blue-eyed, feline sea
sparing its unwitting prey
for a moment of kittenish play.

AMANDA RACHELLE WARREN's work has appeared in *Tusculum Review, The Carolina Quarterly, Appalachian Heritage, Anderbo,* and the *Beloit Poetry Journal,* as well as other journals. Their chapbook *Ritual no.3: For the Exorcism of Ghosts* was published by Stepping Stone Press in 2010. They are the 2017 recipient of the Nickens Poetry Fellowship from the South Carolina Academy of Authors. Their first collection *Rituals for to Call Down Light* was published by Finishing Line Press in 2024. They teach at the University of South Carolina Aiken with their colleague/partner Roy Seeger.

Acknowledgments

"How Many Reasons for This Up and Gone"
    First published in *Fall Lines*
"The Calling"
    First published in *Hearth and Coffin*

Beneath Love Exists Pain

This evening
        sleep is to water as want is to Poor Will singing down the sun.
The pines cain't et our sins away.

                        The light its ownself seems smoke.
Sharp curls rise from the earth

                 but won't yet devour us.
We move in the wake of those many dead.
They ripple against us
        knowing. Want for want.
Stuck for stuck. Pain for pain.

The world seems ruint with language that pools in the way.
So be silent now. Close the door. Bow your head.
Look to love
        ever aware
of what shore pain, like tide, embraces.

Divination Road

Then here you are, come round, thinking I owe you
      what? Saying, *The dead are unreliable.*
And *Get in the car and drive.*

In the cold light of the rearview,
your eyes a cave of wet leaves against passing lights.

You profess the unreliability of the dead,
but here you are, fifteen nights straight
      with your work boots on.

What the dead dream is
spelled in light on the mud-dark water
and mapped in elevation.

And those dreams? Less oracular than mundane,
         take out the dog,
         thaw dinner,
         pay the man what we owe,
         because we do owe.

Twenty-eight miles of mineral silence
before we hit the river road lit
      like a skein of tinsel; one wants

a night of stars for drama's sake.

If I wake in the driveway
      staring at the three-quarter moon,
if I wake in the front passenger's seat of my car
      frosted-over with cold,
or in the kitchen and you've tracked god-knows-what in
      from the other side,

battering my heart with that strong sense of up and leave,
      what might you expect of me? *Baby, get in the car and drive.*

Magnolia, Salt and Pine

I am in love with the heat gathering in the eaves
and what moves from my stepping feet.
I try not to spin in the front yard in a dance for rain.

The dark comes early.
It is 9 pm on the top of the hill and the bright clouds
roll across the state line.
It is 9 pm here and soft dusk drops with spent needles.

How long before we definitively decide it is night?
Because at two a.m. the sky is a smoky purple; at four it oranges up;
dawn is blue and resin-heavy.

Even moonless, the sky is light through the pines
whose lines, extend, threaten to kiss
above my head on a distant plain beyond
whatever sky arrives.
And when they're all backlit and glitter, a cathedral,
their shimmy is the texture of all things.

The old light of stars seems like a threat;
the jangle of legs and wings that strike
and grind, is not music, just bodies in their ripe
exoskeletons.

A fine mist dulls the gloss of magnolia, which except in spring,
is ever composed of separate darks. One leaf shadowed by
all leaves shadowing each other.
Beneath the velvet backs of leaves: egg sacs, patient bodies.

In the dark, things move.

The smell of dirt in the air smothers
the notes of exhaling flowers except
the honeysuckle, magnifying weakness.
I fall asleep in the yard.
I dream of salt. I wake up crying.

How Many Reasons for This Up and Gone

Now the birdbath filled with rain is
                               drawing timid Wills-Widows
          from their hidden branches.

Now the ache centered in the shoulders moves,
                            shifts to the unsutured heart.

Now there seems as though there's a place we're supposed to be,
                            perhaps not here.

Now the dead come;
      their unintelligible whisperings carrying further than soft speech.

Now the many rooms of the house are: a cage
                      are not: a comfort.

Now those lips against my own pulse are my own—
                    what beats feathers there.

Now the road seems honey and coal.

Now the conflicting urges:

     spoon me obligations/lift the barricade on this my waiting life.

The Calling

I am called to shame. The pastor to his affections.

When the faithful open their mouths,
veins pumping with praise, wet to speak,
it is midnight and danger that mingles with love.
And the deep seed of faith is a longing that spoken,
words gliding from the throat uncensored,
would disgrace them all.

That fierce burning settles in the pulse.
Little doors close, so small there. Done.

And one more sweet breakdown bursts forth
like a blossom twisting wet beneath my thumbs.

Or like a gathering of clouds, so low we inhale them.
Or that deep shudder swelling in the chest: press, press.

Oh, insides out everybody.
Scrap that surface which shines.
Or shapes you smooth as sea glass for the taking.
Look at that gleam fall away.

From weakness something subtle comes, but
I will never show you how tender
the skin I kiss on my own wrists. How
charming this shame.

Brother, this is not my life, or this is my life.
And it wants sheets of cold rain brim with ghosts.
And the windows down.
And absolutely blood.
Crossing that soundless baptismal river.

And we are food for angels.
We are food for many things.

Call the body what it is,
a scared and sacred machine, a patchwork of chemicals
held to the light to shine like stained glass, seaming.

Something is swelling to break,
and this machine so numb-tired, so stitched wrong.
Answers.
Obeys.

MARJORY WENTWORTH is the *New York Times* bestselling author of *Out of Wonder: Poems Celebrating Poets* (with Kwame Alexander and Chris Colderley). Her books of poetry include *Noticing Eden, Despite Gravity, The Endless Repetition of an Ordinary Miracle,* and *New and Selected Poems.* She is co-writer of *We Are Charleston: Tragedy and Triumph at Mother Emanuel* (with Herb Frazier and Dr. Bernard Powers) and *Taking a Stand: The Evolution of Human Rights* (with Juan E. Mendez); co-editor of *Seeking: Poetry and Prose Inspired by the Art of Jonathan Green* (with Kwame Dawes); and author of the prizewinning children's story *Shackles.* Wentworth's poems have been nominated for the Pushcart Prize seven times. She was Poet Laureate of South Carolina from 2003-2020 and received the SC Governor's Award for the Arts in 2021. Her archives are held at the James B. Duke Library at Furman University. She was named a Black Earth Institute Fellow for 2022-25. Wentworth teaches at Wright State University.
For further information see marjorywentworth.com.

Acknowledgments

"Hurricane Season"
    First appeared in *Brightleaf, A Southern Review of Books*
"Charleston Rooftops"
    First appeared in *The Dead Mule*
"Holy City" and "One River, One Boat"
    First appeared in *Illuminations*
"Requiem for Rice"
    First appeared in *About Place Journal, Works of Resistance, Resilience* Volume VI, Issue II, October 2020. This poem was written for the Requiem for Rice service at Mother Emanuel AME Church, Charleston, SC 10/22/17.

Hurricane Season

My wound is my geography.
   —Pat Conroy, *The Prince of Tides*

The blood moon thirsts. All night,
listening to unspoken prayers,
she tugs the sea beyond itself
until redundant waves retreating
wash the yellowed marshes clean.

In the heat that follows too much rain,
people crowd the churches.
On this September Sunday morning
their hymns begin to rise
and slap the winds still raging.

This is the music of bones
entwined in mortal language—

words of those who know the wind
erases every footprint carved in earth
where water, tired as a dreamer,
circling beneath oblivious clouds
blurs the variations painted on each human face.

Into the open womb of the sea
descend the ashes of our sins.

What keeps us here? Not gravity
or light, but rust on fences, holding
every house of swollen wood, an ache
a tooth, the day moon adrift
grinding tiny islands down to bone.

Charleston Rooftops

Everything that lifts into the air
has purpose: even the granite tipped war
monument rising above palmetto trees
points like an arrow toward the sun;
chimneys, stove pipes, weathervanes and steeples—
the flag at half mast, flapping in the wind.

Streets clog with memories of smoke-tinged wind—
of a dark sky on fire fueling the air,
flames swirling around steeples,
and a harbor blocked by ships of war.
Cannons fired toward the ever-present sun
until the avenues lined with oak trees

were abandoned, and the trees
thrust transcendent into the wind
reached like prayers toward the sun.
Odors of ruin and rot lingered in the air
above the streets emptied by war;
the bells silent in the steeples.

Beyond scaffold-enshrouded steeples,
sunlight weaves through leaf-thick oak trees
now filled with blossom and song, though war
saturates the brick and memory of wind
spinning with salt through summer air
that simmers beneath the blood-streaked sun.

Red runs through ribbons of sun
across the skyline and steeples
lifting off tin sloped roofs into air
filled with flowering trees.
Always the tireless ocean wind
ripples the worn-out flags of war.

The names of the enemy change, but war
is the inscrutable language spoken beneath this sun.
The flag at half-mast stiffens in the wind.
Funeral bells sound from the steeples.
In the cemetery, beneath the oak trees,
taps linger on the broken air.

The sounds of war will rumble in the wind.
As steeple bells call through the sun-filled air,
birds nest in trees twisting toward heaven.

One River, One Boat

(For Governor Nikki Haley's inauguration Jan. 2015, excluded from inauguration ceremonies, subsequently read into the Congressional Record by Congressman James Clyburn and on the SC Senate floor by Senator Marlon Kimpson.)

I know there's something better down the road.
—Elizabeth Alexander

Because our history is a knot
we try to unravel, while others
try to tighten it, we tire easily
and fray the cords that bind us.

The cord is a slow-moving river,
spiraling across the land
in a succession of S's,
splintering near the sea.

Picture us all, crowded onto a boat
at the last bend in the river:
watch children stepping off the school bus,
parents late for work, grandparents

fishing for favorite memories,
teachers tapping their desks
with red pens, firemen suiting up
to save us, nurses making rounds,

baristas grinding coffee beans,
dockworkers unloading apartment-size
containers of computers and toys
from factories across the sea.

Every morning a different veteran
stands at the base of the bridge
holding a cardboard sign
with misspelled words and an empty cup.

In fields at daybreak, rows of migrant
farm workers standing on ladders, break open
iced peach blossoms; their breath rising
and resting above the frozen fields like clouds.

A jonboat drifts down the river.
Inside, a small boy lies on his back;
hand laced behind his head, he watches
stars fade from the sky and dreams.

Consider the prophet John, calling us
from the edge of the wilderness to name
the harm that has been done, to make it
plain, and enter the river and rise.

It is not about asking for forgiveness.
It is not about bowing our heads in shame;
because it all begins and ends here:
while workers unearth trenches

at Gadsden's Wharf, where 100,000
Africans were imprisoned within brick walls
awaiting auction, death, or worse.
Where the dead were thrown into the water,

and the river clogged with corpses
has kept centuries of silence.
It is time to gather at the edge of the sea,
and toss wreaths into this watery grave.

And it is time to praise the judge
who cleared George Stinney's name,
seventy years after the fact,
we honor him; we pray.

Here, where the Confederate flag
flies beside the Statehouse, haunted
by our past, conflicted about the future;
at the heart of it, we are at war with ourselves

huddled together on this boat
handed down to us—stuck
at the last bend of a wide river
splintering near the sea.

In memory of Walter Scott and Muhiyyidin d'Baha

Holy City

Only love can conquer hate.
—Reverend Clementa Pinckney

Let us gather and be
silent together like stones
glittering in sunlight

so bright it hurts our eyes
emptied of tears and searching
the sky for answers.

Let us be strangers
together as we gather
in circles wherever we meet,

to stand hand in hand and sing
hymns to the heavens and pray
for the fallen and speak their names:

Clementa, Cynthia, Tywanza,
Ethel, Sharonda, Daniel,
Myra, Susie and Depayne.

They are not alone. As bells
in the spires call across
the wounded Charleston sky,

we close our eyes and listen
to the same stillness ringing
in our hearts, holding onto

one another like brothers,
like sisters because we know
wherever there is love, there is God.

Requiem for Rice

for Jonathan Green

When we walk from the sea
Along the river
Filling with tides,
We will bend down
To plant rice in mud
That was here before
We came. Water
Touching roots, growing
Beyond memory.

We will pass
Neglected
Graves
Of the enslaved.
The earth holds
Their names
The way it holds rain.

We will dig through
Centuries until
We find them,
Bent to earth
Bent to water
We will plant rice
Beyond the numbers
Beyond the names.

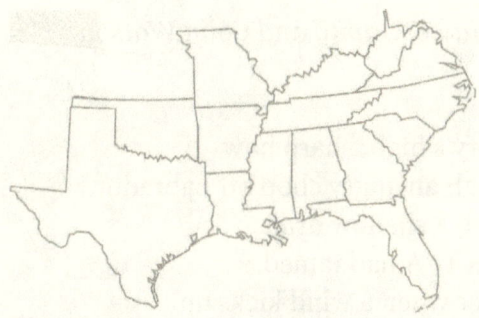

EDWARD WILSON was born in Muhlenberg County, Kentucky (famed of Merle Travis, the Everly Brothers, John Prine's song "Paradise," Warren Oates, and, for many decades of the last century, coal, lots of coal). His poems are anthologized and have appeared in the *American Poetry Review, Beloit Poetry Journal, The Georgia Review, The Midwest Quarterly, Narrative Magazine, Poetry* (Chicago), *The Southern Poetry Review*, and others. His awards include an NEA fellowship, a Bread Loaf Writers Conference Fellowship, and an Individual Artist grant from the state of Georgia. His collection, *In a Rich Country*, won the 2019 Grayson Books Poetry Prize and was the finalist for Georgia Author of the Year in 2020. He has lived in Augusta, Georgia, since 1982.

The Boat

for Bob, Judie, Gavin, and Colin Watson

Clean lines. A dory's high, sharp bow
for cutting through an angry chop off Labrador,
but flat-bottomed, a shallow draft
for the local lakes TVA had tamed.
A cabin for shelter when a wind kicks up.
Cockpit enough to hold the souls of us
who showed up each Thanksgiving.
Brightwork gleaming. Every bare rail varnished.
In the side yard on its trailer under the tarp
the weekend I drove up.

      It was so unexpected

since he'd never mentioned it and for years
we'd hardly missed a week without a talk,
what we did best. It was as unlikely
as an actuary moonlighting as a farrier
for a man so comfortable with any page of words.

I wondered how the plans had caught him,
why he drove more than a 100 miles
for an engine they no longer made.
He must have worked more than a year
in that bare space he'd found to lease—cutting,
planing, sanding—glue and caulk and paint.
Correcting, he said, yesterday's mistakes.

I meant to get his thoughts—what he'd bought
with all those hours spent—
but things came up, the way they always did,
each time we'd planned to take it out.

A boat is like a Rorschach—many things
to many men. Pride of accomplishment.
Mastery of skills. An excuse for time alone.
Peace of mind, perhaps. And waiting, unused,
but ready where it sits.

A lawn is comforting—the way from porches
it will stretch predictably away toward
the ridgeline below the morning sky.
No nightmarish monstrous wave enraged
by winds across 1000 miles of open ocean
rising to break, intent on splintering the house.

But calms are temporary. Weather is change.
Under the clearest skies, on land far firmer
than a glassy sea, people will go missing,
are swept overboard and lost.

       I didn't ask until he couldn't answer.

But I remember that last Christmas:
Judie's oven making luscious promises—
him on the couch, cheering the Gators,
rooting for the Bulls—grandsons, those two boys,
caroming round the room.

       It was for them.

The Long View

for Preston and Shari

This morning, we've passed
a patch of grass beside the creek
where his grandfather built and ran
a store, twisted a ways up a road,
parked and found the weedy track,
choked with brush and deadfall,
to the burying ground—half
the size of a tennis court—hacked
vine and briar away until, by noon,
we've found the stones. A dozen
and a half. Sagging, tipped, some
fallen, broken. The poorest crumbled
like loaves of stale bread. And
scattered in between, around,
more stoneless plots. Dips, shallows
in the earth, like prints of thumbs
in dough, that catch the leaves.

He and his wife do this
a few times every year. Before
they leave this or that small place
he'll find the stone least legible,
weathered smooth as an old man's
memory, jot the name and date,
take it to the carver. And when
it's done, bring it back and set it up
where the old one was.

He doesn't farm much anymore,
puts in a garden every spring,
mows the field along the road
when it seems to need it. Trees
have his attention now. He'll cut
one now and then, sell the board

or make a table or a cabinet
in his shop.

This afternoon,
around the hill, across the field,
beyond the barn, we walk his back
woodlot. Kicking through the leaves,
we don't say much. We've known
each other close to 60 years. We've
said most of what we have to say.
For him, these woods are like a
family. He knows these trees like
cousins. He stops in front of one—
a walnut, thicker that a phone pole
and my waist.

In 50 years, he says,
there'll be some good wood there.

Sometimes a Day Gets Lost

wanders away from April
maybe or late September.
It arrives without papers, itself
its own passport. In gutters
leaves are confused. What was
escape is play. It is enough
to make trees dream erupting
green. Out of the blue, light
falls through crystal, soft,
breeze nuzzling everything.

An equal opportunity miracle
like some ripe galleon blown
off course, split open on a reef,
scatters glittering tonnage
over the sand or the way you
wandered along that street one
afternoon into the little shop,
chock-a-block with nothing
you'd ever want, lifted something
from a shelf and looked at me.

Ruby

High School Reunion
for Forrest Mallory and John Hill Neeley

"I'm so glad to see you, Honey!
Tell me, what's the best you know?"
She asks, quits pulling weeds
and, happy as a girl, sits on the stone
swinging a worn-out running shoe
right over where she'll lie between
her husband and her son, my friend,
who half my life ago, this week,
moved here.

　　　By accident. By chance.

The way I'm here. And as we talk
I know she'll get around to telling
how no mark was on him when
the car rolled to a stop. And we will see,
tonight, my good blond friend, who drove.
I'd speak for him—for all of us who
never met mistakes we didn't make.
Whose faults like loose change
on the dresser compound overnight.

　　　But what's to say?

He that is without sin among you
let him cast a stone? Sufficient
unto the day is the evil thereof?
Why seek ye the living among the dead?
The best thing I know, Ruby, is the sky
this afternoon. And how it clears.
And the maple leaves, yellow and wet,
half on the trees, half spread out
on the ground. The way they smell.

COVER ARTIST

A BFA graduate of Augusta University with a specialization in painting, **MICHAEL BUDD** has recently focused his creative attention on plein air subjects, including a series of works that he calls "drive-by landscapes" because they take their inspiration from images captured via camera through the windshields or side windows of moving vehicles. One such landscape is the oil painting that graces the cover of this volume: *Pine Log Road*, which so aptly represents the trajectory of this anthology as it takes readers on a lyrical journey across the South. A longtime favorite of private collectors, the artwork of Michael Budd has also been featured in group exhibitions in Georgia and South Carolina and on the covers and pages of a number of academic and commercial publications.

EDITORS

TOM MACK holds the rank of USC Distinguished Professor Emeritus. During his thirty-nine years on the faculty of the University of South Carolina Aiken, twenty-five of those years as chair of the English Department, he was frequently recognized for his teaching, scholarship, and public service. In 2008, the USC Board of Trustees awarded him the prestigious Carolina Trustee Professorship; and in 2014, he received the Governor's Award in the Humanities. Besides writing numerous articles on American cultural history for various academic journals and reference volumes, Dr. Mack was also the founding editor of *The Oswald Review*, the first international refereed journal of undergraduate research in the discipline of English. He is the author of four books: *Circling the Savannah*, *Hidden History of Aiken County*, *Hidden History of Augusta*, and *100 Things to Do in Augusta, Georgia Before You Die*. Mack also edited *The South Carolina Encyclopedia Guide to South Carolina Writers* and two short story collections, *Dancing on Barbed Wire* and *Magic, Mystery, and Madness: electric ekphrastics*. With Andrew Geyer, he co-edited the award-winning composite anthology *A Shared Voice*. For over thirty years, he has also written a weekly "Arts and Humanities" column in *The Aiken Standard* and for over a dozen years has served on the board of the South Carolina Academy of Authors, which manages the state's literary hall of fame.

ANDREW GEYER's tenth book is *Magic, Mystery, Madness: electric ekphrastics,* a co-authored composite anthology. His individually authored books are the story cycles *Lesser Mountains, Siren Songs from the Heart of Austin,* and *Whispers in Dust and Bone*; and the novels *Dixie Fish* and *Meeting the Dead*. Geyer's other co-authored books are the hybrid story cycles *Dancing on Barbed Wire* and *Texas 5X5,* and the novel *Parallel Hours*. He also co-edited the composite anthology *A Shared Voice* with Tom Mack. Honors for Geyer's fiction include an IPPY, an INDIE, and two Spur Awards. A member of the Texas Institute of Letters and the South Carolina Academy of Authors, he currently serves as English Department Chair at the University of South Carolina Aiken and Managing Editor at *The Petrigru Review*.